Early Childhood Education
It's an Art?
It's a Science?

Outstanding Presentations

from the

NAEYC 1975 Annual Conference

Library of Congress Catalog Card Number: 76-6011

ISBN Catalog Number: 0-912674-48-2

Printed in the United States of America.

Early Childhood Education
It's an Art?
It's a Science?

J. D. Andrews, Editor
NAEYC Conference Director

The National Association for the Education of Young Children
Washington, D.C.

Contents

Introduction

If you feel comfortable with the state of the "art" and "science" of early childhood education as it is practiced, researched, and reported today, read no further. The ideas between the covers of this book come from, and are addressed to, people who are struggling and willing to experience dissonance in order to become more skillful in improving the quality of growth-supporting services available to children and their families in this country. Within this potpourri of thought-stimulators, you will encounter ideas that set your thinking spinning—ideas you had previously dealt with now stated in a new way, and ideas that upset you.

Approximately 8,000 people met in Dallas, Texas, in November of 1975 to examine "Early Childhood Education: It's an Art? It's a Science?" For most conferees, the experience reconfirmed that early childhood education is inseparably grounded in both the arts and the sciences. The real purpose of this theme was to sensitize us to the enormous complexity of early childhood development and education and to help us recognize and combat the tendency to withdraw to a narrowly focused, one-disciplined point of reference. It is understandable that we retreat to the disciplines of knowledge we are most familiar with and biased toward, but in doing so we commit a grave disservice to children. Many of today's unsolved problems in achieving quality programs for young people are caused by simplistic, non-discipline-integrated thinking.

In his opening conference address Ed Zigler credited NAEYC members with a performance record of putting the best interests of young children above other interests. If NAEYC is to maintain the interests of children as our first priority, we must expand our thinking about children to integrate many sources of knowledge into a more nearly accurate picture of these beautifully complex young human beings who will determine this nation's tomorrow.

Marilyn M. Smith
Executive Director, NAEYC

Head Start: Not a Program but an Evolving Concept

Edward Zigler, *Professor of Psychology; Head, Psychology Section, Child Study Center, Yale University, New Haven, Connecticut.*

This is an extremely difficult period for those of us committed to child development programs, particularly programs directed at optimizing the development of economically-disadvantaged children. It seems we are being attacked on all sides, both by individuals who probably share our values concerning the importance of child development programs and by those whose values and priorities are different from our own.

On the one hand we have the attack of the hereditarians (e.g., Jensen, Herrnstein, Eysenck) who have argued that compensatory efforts must fail since genetic factors are such overriding determinants of human behavior. In several analytic papers (Zigler 1970, 1973, 1975), I have taken exception to this indictment, and have questioned whether such conclusions concerning the potential value of compensatory programs actually flow unerringly from the data presented by Jensen and others concerning genetic effects on human intelligence. I do not think they do and have argued that the nature-nurture controversy concerning the phenotypic expression of intelligence is essentially irrelevant to the issue of whether or not compensatory programs are of value.

This point can be made relatively simply. As Cronbach (1969) has noted, even if we ac-

1

cept Jensen's estimate that the heritability index for intelligence is .80 (and many of course do not, feeling this figure is an inflated one), this would mean that the reaction range for the phenotypic expression of intelligence is about 25 IQ points. Stated somewhat differently, this means that there can be a 25-point difference in intelligence test performance by the same individual subjected to the worst possible environment as opposed to the best possible environment. Since, even using Jensen's estimates, we can theoretically improve through environmental manipulations (such as our compensatory education efforts) children's IQ performance by as much as 25 points, this raises the question of whether IQ changes of this magnitude are worth our time and effort.

The question here revolves around the troublesome issue of statistical versus practical significance. Whatever a statistically reliable difference in IQ might be, we still have to ask how much change in IQ is required for us to assert that our effort was practically significant. I am indebted to Sheldon White (1970) of Harvard for pointing out that educators have adopted the convention of treating as of practical consequence changes in test performance having a magnitude one-half as large as the standard deviation of the test. Since the standard deviation of our IQ tests is approximately 16, this would mean that a change in IQ of approximately 8 points would signal a practically significant and worthwhile intervention effort. The most constant finding in the compensatory education literature is a 10-point increase in IQ, whatever type of program the child experienced. This means that even if one adopted the narrowest and most stringent assessment criteria, one would have to conclude that compensatory education is an impressive success.

In addition to the hereditarians, indictments of the value of compensatory education programs have now come from a number of learned investigators who can hardly be considered hostile toward preschool intervention efforts. I am thinking here of the analytic papers and assessments of preschool compensatory education which have appeared in recent years by such individuals as Carl Bereiter (1972), Herbert Ginsburg (1972), Larry Kohlberg (1968), and Sheldon White (1970).

Reading this critical but nonetheless responsible literature has convinced me that we have in the past adopted, or at least appeared to have adopted, theroetic and programmatic positions which are in error. We must not be so concerned with our image that we fail to disavow our theoretical presuppositions once these presuppositions have been demonstrated to be erroneous. We must purge the compensatory education field, especially its bellwether—Head Start—of the theoretical excesses and fallacious views of the mid-sixties. I agree with Bettye Caldwell's (1974) assertion that at the time of the inception of Head Start we were overly optimistic concerning the amount of effort required to produce permanent changes in the quality of children's behavior, and that such overoptimism had to invariably give way to the pessimism that now confronts us.

Allow me to jog your memory. In reaction to the Gesellians and other proponents of the fixed IQ, Joe Hunt, Ben Bloom, and others constructed for us a theoretical view which conceptualized the young child as possessing an almost unlimited degree of plasticity. As late as 1971, Joe Hunt continued to assert that the norm of reaction for intelligence was 70 IQ points (rather than Cronbach's more reasonable estimate of 25 points) and that relatively short-term intervention efforts could result in IQ gains of 48 or 63 points. With such environmental sugarplums dancing in our heads, we actually thought that we could compensate for the effects of several years of impoverishment as well as inoculate the child against the future ravages of such impoverishment, all by providing a six- or eight-week summer Head Start experience. It should surprise no one to hear that we soon found such minimal efforts to be relatively ineffective. It is just not that easy.

It is now my view that such tokenistic programs probably are worse than no programs at all. The danger in tokenistic efforts is not so much that they damage children as that they give the appearance that something useful is being done and thus become the substitute for more meaningful efforts. Children have the right to the best programs we are capable of mounting, and we should all join ranks in opposing tokenism which allows our society to evade its responsibility to those children who need our help the most.

Since positions suffering from theoretical excesses always appear to give rise to opposing excessive positions, it should come as no surprise to note that the naive environmentalism of the 1960s now is being attacked by the neomaturationist views of one of America's most thoughtful developmentalists, Jerome Kagan of Harvard.

In addition to naive environmentalism and its corollary, the almost limitless plastic child, another error is badly in need of correction. I am thinking here of the cognitive emphasis in so many of our compensatory education evaluation efforts. We should have never allowed the IQ score to become the ultimate indicator of compensatory education's success or failure. The goal of Head Start never was to produce a cadre of geniuses to man the teaching posts at our universities. We should reduce the confusion that I now see in this area by clearly and openly asserting that the goal of Head Start is the production of socially competent human beings. We should make clear to everyone that cognitive functioning is just one of several criteria that must be employed in the definition of social competence. When the history of compensatory education in the 1960s is finally written, it will be reported that our early efforts embraced a cognitive emphasis tied to a naive environmentalism. My argument here today has been that both of these tenets must be repudiated.

Once we evaluate Head Start in terms of appropriate rather than inappropriate criteria, we will discover that Head Start has been far more successful than its critics would have us believe. Let us examine the record.

I continue to be surprised and disappointed that the health and nutrition aspects of Head Start are almost totally ignored in formal assessments of the program done to date. Approximately one-third of the children attending Head Start have been found to have identifiable physical defects, and about 75 percent of such defects have been treated. We thus see that over the years Head Start has been our nation's largest deliverer of health services to poor children.

Also underappreciated is Head Start's pioneering effort in parent involvement. From its inception to the present time Head Start has been a model in not only demonstrating that parental participation can be done, but also that it is worth doing. In a recent discussion, Seymour Sarason, my colleague at Yale, expressed the view that the single greatest accomplishment of social action programs of the 1960s may prove to be the development of a cadre of socially involved leaders among minority groups and among the economically disadvantaged, groups that history tells us have been almost powerless in influencing the nature and quality of their own lives. Head Start has led the way in this important social development.

Does the development of such a cadre of leaders among the Head Start constituency have value for children? I believe that it does. Ed Gordon of Columbia, in an insightful paper (1971), intimated how the development of leadership potential among the poor might be an important factor in optimizing children's development. In taking exception to the newly emerging conventional wisdom that variations in schooling make little difference in variations in the intellectual and personality development of children, Gordon pointed out a finding in the Coleman report (1966) that has gone relatively unnoticed: namely, that with the exception of family background, the variable most related to school performance was the child's sense of control of the world the child inhabits.

How does the child's sense of control develop? The modeling formulations of Bandura and others instruct us that children will develop the world view that they can influence their own destiny if they have the opportunity to interact with adult models who themselves feel that what they do makes a difference in influencing their environment. I believe that such an outlook is supported by Head Start's parent involvement effort. I therefore conclude that a commitment to parental involvement leads relatively quickly to positive attitudes among children that must be nurtured before school performance can become optimal.

Somewhat related to the parental involvement phenomenon is the success Head Start has had in improving services to children. When Head Start was conceived we hoped that this program would be an important institutional change agent in improving the lives of children not only during the Head Start years but in those years before and after the child's participation in Head Start. How successful has Head Start been in regard to such a goal? It has been more successful than many people know.

I would like to call your attention to the Kirschner report (1970) which looked at health and education services to children in approximately 50 communities having Head Start programs as contrasted with several communities which did not have Head Start. In the Head Start communities, over 1,500 identifiable incidents were documented in the improved delivery of health and educational services to poor children. Nothing approaching this record was found in the non-Head Start communities. Why does everyone quote the Westinghouse report (1969), which allegedly definitively demonstrates the failure of Head Start, while no one notes the Kirschner report, which documents clearly the success of Head Start?

Another major accomplishment of Head Start has been placing well over ten thousand unemployed and underemployed poor people into college programs to permit these individuals to pursue professional roles in child care programs. Such an accomplishment is a major one inasmuch as our nation currently does not have a large enough cadre of caretakers to provide services for children already in child care programs, to say nothing of the much larger number of such professionals which will be required as we expand our child care services in America.

Let us now ask the central question. Do children who experience Head Start manifest greater gains on cognitive and personality measures that do comparison children who have not had the Head Start experience? The answer to this question is a resounding "Yes." Why then has it become fashionable to speak of the failure of Head Start? The assertion of Head Start's failure is based upon the reported finding that the advantage of Head Start children over non-Head Start children is not maintained once the children have spent two or three years in elementary school. But how is this finding to be interpreted? The raw data would appear to represent more an indictment of schools rather than of Head Start.

I would like to issue a serious warning against the popular "fade out" notion. That is, the current conventional wisdom concerning the impact of Head Start is that the gains in performance obtained by Head Start children as compared to non-Head Start controls fade out a year or two into the elementary school grades. My own considered views concerning this bit of conventional wisdom are that it is more conventional then it is wise. From the Wolff and Steiner report (n.d.) through the Westinghouse report (1969) to Bronfenbrenner's scholarly analysis conducted for OCD (1974), we have been informed that there are no striking long-term effects accruing from a one-year Head Start experience. This has been repeated so often that many now treat this conclusion as beyond question. I choose to question it. In flocking to this position, thinkers have ignored a relatively large and consistent body of evidence which indicates that the benefits of participating in a preschool intervention program have much greater staying power than currently popular views would have us believe. For those of you who are not prepared to accept that there are discernible effects accruing from experiencing the Head Start program, I recommend that you read a recently prepared review of the evidence on this point written by Frank Palmer (1975). I assert here today that besides being erroneous, the worst danger of the "fadeout" position is that it provides ammunition to those in America who feel that expending money in an effort to improve the lives of economically-disadvantaged children is a waste.

I do not wish to appear to be inconsistent. Nothing that I have said on the fadeout issue should be misconstrued as being in opposition to my earlier voiced awareness of the inherent dangers involved in overselling what can be accomplished through not very intensive programs of relatively short duration. All that I am doing is asking decision makers not to set social policy on the basis of the conclusion that there are no long-term effects of Head Start attendance. I say to these decision makers that the evidence on this point is not as unidirectional as many currently believe. Bad science makes for bad social policy. I ask my colleagues in the research community to forego the temptation of delivering definitive pronouncements concerning the fadeout issue and await instead the collection and analyses of more data. Such a stance strikes me as currently being the only reasonable one if thinkers are to combine social responsibility with the researchers' deeply ingrained attitudes of skepticism and objectivity.

I have now spent a decade reading the results of studies investigating the effects of early childhood interventions. (As you know, evaluating intervention programs has become something of a cottage industry among psychologists and psychometricians.) What does all this work show and what directions does it give to our future efforts in aiding children? After digesting all of this data, I have come to the conclusion that once again science has labored mightily to demonstrate the obvious. Ignoring the fadeout issue, any rational reading of this literature forces one to concur with Urie Bronfenbrenner (1974) and Sally Ryan (1974), both of whom mined the same terrain. Their conclusions taken together indicate there are two factors that are critical in determining the success of preschool intervention efforts: (1) getting parents involved in the training of their own children and (2) guaranteeing that schools follow the Head Start program with further compensatory efforts.

It was our growing awareness of the value of training parents to work with their own children rather than training the children apart from their families which gave rise to the Home Start program. Just as I consider the Home Start effort to be a wave of the future, I also think OCD's Child and Family Resource Centers are most promising and innovative. These centers guarantee the dovetailing of programs across the life cycle and thus provide continuous intervention during the early childhood years.

I am troubled by the current tendency, even on the part of certain knowledgeable workers, to conceptualize Head Start as though it were the same program that we initiated a decade ago. We may have become the victims of our own evaluation procedures inasmuch as these procedures deal best with static programs which involve a homogeneously administered treatment condition. The thousand Head Start centers certainly do not represent a homogeneous treatment condition. There is probably as much variation within Head Start as there is between Head Start and non-Head Start environments. Furthermore, Head Start is not a static program. The true meaning of Head Start is that it is an evolving concept. Many of us have witnessed this evolution. As empirical evidence came in from a variety of sources, we examined this evidence for its social action implications and devised a family of programs which taken together currently define Head Start. They are:

1. Parent and Child Centers
2. Parent and Child Advocacy Centers
3. Follow Through Program
4. Planned Variation Program

5. Head Start Handicapped Children's Effort
6. Health Start
7. Home Start
8. Head Start Improvement and Innovation Effort
9. Head Start Continuity Effort
10. Child and Family Resource Program
11. Child Development Associate Program
12. Education for Parenthood Program

As I look at this family of programs I must conclude that we have probably allowed our programmatic efforts to outdistance our evaluation efforts. At one level such a state of affairs can be troublesome to the scientific purists among us. I personally do not find this state of affairs particularly troublesome since I firmly believe that rigorous evaluation is the servant of social policy and not its master. On the other hand, this state of affairs does force social policy people to do some serious soul-searching concerning the role of research and evaluation in constructing social policy. As a behavioral scientist committed to the empirical tradition, I will continue to champion the value of research and program assessment in aiding the policymaker in the decision-making function, especially in those instances when difficult choices must be made between competing program alternatives.

Head Start is a classic example of a program whose development quickly outdistanced its empirical and evaluative base. In the first summer of Head Start, it was the expectation of the planning committee (chaired by Robert Cooke) that approximately 100,000 children would enter the program. At that time we developed some admittedly crude evaluation techniques. Thus, from its inception the Head Start philosophy included a commitment to objective evaluation so that we might properly assess the effects of this program so hurriedly put into place. As you know, instead of 100,000 children, the first summer of Head Start saw 500,000 children entered into the program.This unexpectedly large number was both gratifying and frightening to the planning committee which was charged with developing the rationale and broad programmatic directions of the Head Start effort.

The planning committee engaged in considerable discussion on the issue of what was the optimal size for the Head Start program in its first summer of life. One point of view was that the original Head Start program be a small, closely monitored effort which would be carefully evaluated and later expanded, provided the evaluation clearly indicated that the children benefited from participation in the program. This would have been a conservative and defensible position. However, such a course of action struck the planning committee as making evaluation the master rather than the servant of social policy. When the planning committee obtained a clear signal that the decision makers who had the clout wished to commit very large amounts of money to the Head Start program, they seized the moment and endorsed the decision to expand greatly Head Start before any evaluation findings had been collected.

What factors led us to such a risky decision? They include: (1) We were caught up in the environmental mystique of the mid-sixties and probably were overly impressed with those preschool intervention efforts which predated the Head Start program. However, the planning committee did have some reservations that an eight-week program would have substantial effects. (2) There was no evidence that such a program would have negative consequences. (We employed the dictum, "Primum non nocere" [first not to injure].) Indeed, if we did nothing more than provide a half-million children with badly needed health services, the Head Start program in its summer of 1965 form appeared worth doing. (3) The whole experience of planning Head Start was a rather heady one conducted by individuals who for the most part had little or no experience of having decision makers take their views seriously enough to back such views with hundreds of millions of dollars. This was a seductive state of affairs in which reservations and caution were likely to be ignored.

This bit of history raises an interesting question. Thanks to the efforts of such workers as Campbell (1969), we have become much more sophisticated in developing methods to evaluate programs such as Head Start. However, this enhanced methodological ability is essentially silent in regard to an important social policy issue, namely, what are the appropriate ground rules for determining when it is appropriate (and when it is not) to begin or expand programs before any convincing evaluative data are available. My hunch is that the answer to this question will not be illuminated by individuals whose concerns are essentially of the methodological-statistical type. The personality literature on human traits provides us with some relevant evidence concerning the issue. I'm thinking here of the literature on risktaking. While the planning committee of Head Start was probably not sufficiently sensitive to all the risks of Head Start, we knew we were taking a calculated risk. We had little in the way of information or methodology to guide us. In taking the risk we did, on the positive side, we saw the possibility of producing happier, healthier, and more socially competent children. On the negative side we saw only the waste of some money. I concur that we also were probably not sufficiently sensitive to the value and importance of money. How could any group meeting at a time when the nation was spending billions on an unpopular war in Southeast Asia be very concerned about wasting a few hundred million on improving the lives of our nation's economically-disadvantaged children?

As I have stated in another context (1975), I now believe that such an attitude was little more than a cop-out. The real problem is not in deciding between Head Start and a war in Southeast Asia. The real problem is in deciding on how to allocate an always finite number of dollars to competing programs—all directed at optimizing the development of children. I would make the plea that behavioral scientists working at the intersect of knowledge and social policy get to work immediately in developing a psychology of the calculated risk. How should social policy decisions be made? A corollary question here would be, how might we best develop cost-benefit models to aid us in selecting between social policy alternatives. (See Zigler 1973 for a discussion of the great difficulty involved in constructing such cost-benefit equations.)

I find myself essentially in agreement with the views of one of America's most thoughtful analysts, Donald Campbell of Northwestern University. Allow me to quote briefly from Campbell (1969):

> The United States and other modern nations should be ready for an experimental approach to social reform, an approach in which we try out new programs designed to cure specific social problems, in which we learn whether or not these programs are effective, and in which we retain, imitate, modify, or discard them on the basis of apparent effectiveness on the multiple imperfect criteria available. (p. 409)

I assert that Head Start has been a model of the way in which Campbell feels that society should proceed.

What then of the future of Head Start? We shall continue with a variety of efforts and adopt and expand those which appear to hold promise. My best hunch is that over the next decade the concept of a Head Start program will be replaced by the concept of the Head Start center involving a variety of programs. Hopefully these programs will be made available to the child on the basis of the child's needs rather than on the basis of our preconceptions.

The view that economically-disadvantaged children are a homogeneous group of children universally in need of a single type of intervention program is also a vestige of the erroneous thinking of the 1960s. Does every poor child need a year of Head Start? These children are a heterogeneous group with a variety of needs. Let us finally state openly and clearly that many of these children, like their more affluent middle SES peers, have perfectly adequate homes and are in no serious need of a compensatory or preventive program. Others need a one-year Head Start program, others a two-year program, others just a play group. Some handicapped children need a program from birth to age eight and then more. Let's tailor programs to the needs of children rather than mindlessly fitting children to a particular program conceptualized as some panacea to be experienced by each and every child who happens to be in a home where the family income is below some arbitrary dollar amount. Categorizing children on the basis of family income is counterproductive, since such a grouping procedure does not produce groups of children who are homogeneous in regard to psychological characteristics and thus homogeneous in regard to the need for a particular type of intervention.

This is a difficult time for workers committed to mounting social action programs for children. This is a difficult time for both you and me. You will need all of the courage and resiliency that you are capable of if you are to continue fighting the good fight.

I believe the remarks I have made to you, or I would not have made them. I feel most of them very strongly. But it is time for me to put aside prepared speeches and instead talk to you in a way that a friend would talk to another. Honesty demands that I say I am not sufficiently recovered from my recent illness to be able to articulate as well as I would like, and I really did not want to come and deliver a dense talk of the sort I just delivered to you. I had to ask myself: I'll see a lot of friends at NAEYC, that's reason enough for coming, but why come out on the platform to do that? I came out on the platform this evening not to deliver the talk I just presented, but rather to tell you something about NAEYC and what it means to me.

NAEYC has been my security blanket for several years. I owe this organization more than I could ever repay. My own professional career has been intimately involved with your organization, and that is why I decided to be here and to tell you briefly about Ed Zigler and his views on NAEYC. I still remember the first speech I gave when I become our nation's first Director of the Office of Child Development. It was a speech at your Boston national conference, and it was a very tense time. I did not know whether I would be able to speak or not. There was going to be a demonstration, there were police, and there was going to be physical violence—it was a difficult period.

Just before coming on the platform somebody handed me a recent issue of *U.S. News and World Report* and said, "Hey, Ed, have you seen this? Look at it before you go on." So I opened it up and there it was: The always unnamed, high level White House person had announced that we all know Head Start is a failure; it is just a babysitting service for welfare mothers. Well this is what I was armed with to take over the job at the Office of Child Development. There should have been a demonstration against me and what I represented.

I was asked, "How do you want to handle it?" We thought it would make sense to have the people there who were concerned about what I was going to do question me so I could reply. That is still the NAEYC way. Let people have their say, give me a chance to have mine, and it proved to be a very interesting episode.

These people had very legitimate concerns, and I don't know if any of those individuals who questioned me closely are here in the audience, but I'm very grateful to that group of people. Over the next two years of my life in Washington several of those people who put me on the griddle helped me time and time again. I don't know if I was able to teach them anything in two years, but I do want to say thanks to NAEYC again for providing the hall; they sure taught me a lot. I will always be grateful to them.

Again, I can remember that the questioning got to be a little unfair. I guess I was accused of supporting some design to cut back the Social Security program, to increase the war in Vietnam. Clearly I was just standing there as the object for any grievance that anybody possibly could have. Evelyn Omwake, a friend and a past president of NAEYC, came forward and said, "Enough. You had something to say and Dr. Zigler had the opportunity to answer you. What's positive and constructive has been done. Now let's allow him to leave." And she put her arm around me, and Milt Akers came forward, and they literally spirited me out of the hall because there was still this terrible fear that some physical harm would befall me. Milt Akers is no longer with us, but he will live on in my memory and in yours, and perhaps most importantly he will live on in the many accomplishments in which he played a role, accomplishments that made the lives of children in this nation better. He was a wonderful man.

I want to tell you that NAEYC has a decided penchant for selecting outstanding executive directors. I have never been prouder of a colleague than I was of Marilyn Smith in Washington a few months ago when the first CDAs were awarded. The CDA is a very complicated effort that a lot of people have different goals for; they see it as accomplishing different things. I was so relieved and so gratified when at that presentation Marilyn Smith stepped forward and in one sentence brought clarity out of chaos. She said the CDA is an effort to make the lives of children better. And she was right; she said it simply, eloquently, and well. But in that statement she said something about NAEYC too.

I am worried about the CDA effort and its future. I am of course delighted to have a stalwart, another past president of NAEYC, Evangeline Ward, at the throttle. She is a magnificent person who will do as well with that program as any human being possibly could. But what delights me about NAEYC's role in the CDA effort was you weren't protecting the turf for yourselves, you weren't looking to your own self interests. It was easy to be for CDA back in 1972 when we had an expanding economy and no serious teacher unemployment. But I have noticed that since times have gotten a little tougher we now have some people who are dropping away from the CDA effort.

I can say one thing about NAEYC. Never have I seen you falter by putting your own best interest first. To my knowledge you have, upon many occasions, worked against your best interests, supporting instead the best interests of young children.

I must say to you, I am not sure yet how this is all going to come out. I have been 20 years now working at advocacy for children. Sometimes I really wonder if the good guys are ever going to win. And it frightens me, but then I think about NAEYC. That is what I meant about your being my security blanket. Some of us might fall by the wayside, but NAEYC, I am sure, will never quit.

The next two or three years are going to be very tough years for us all. They are going to require every bit of courage that each and every one of you has to keep your resolve high, and even after we suffer a defeat or two, to roll up your sleeves and get right back into the fray. It is that kind of commitment, that kind of courage that is NAEYC to me, and I am here tonight just to say one thing. Thank you for myself and thank you for children.

References

Bereiter, C. "An Academic Preschool for Disadvantaged Children: Conclusions for Evaluation Studies." In *Preschool Programs for the Disadvantaged: Five Experimental Approaches to Early Childhood Education,* edited by J.C. Stanley, pp. 1-21. Baltimore: Johns Hopkins University Press, 1972.

Bronfenbrenner, U. *A Report on Longitudinal Evaluations of Preschool Programs.* Vol. 2. *Is Early Intervention Effective?* Washington, D.C.: Department of Health, Education, and Welfare, 1974. Publication No. (OHD) 74-25.

Caldwell, B.M. "A Decade of Early Intervention Programs: What We Have Learned." *American Journal of Orthopsychiatry* 44 (1974): 491-496.

Campbell, D. "Reforms as Experiments." *American Psychologist* 24 (1969): 409-429.

Coleman, J., et al. *Equality of Educational Opportunity.* Washington, D.C.: U.S. Government Printing Office, 1966.

Cronbach, L.J. "Heredity, Environment, and Educational Policy."*Harvard Educational Review* 39 (Spring 1969): 338-347.

Ginsburg, H. *The Myth of the Deprived Child: Poor Children's Intellect and Education.* Englewood Cliffs, N.J.: Prentice-Hall, 1972.

Gordon, E. "Parent and Child Centers: Their Basis in the Behavioral and Educational Sciences—An Invited Critique." *American Journal of Orthopsychiatry* 41 (1971): 39-42.

Kirschner Associates, Inc. *A National Survey of the Impacts of Head Start Centers on Community Institutions.* Albuquerque, N. Mex.: Kirschner Associates, Inc., May 1970.

Kohlberg, L. "Early Education: A Cognitive Developmental View." *Child Development* 39 (1968): 1013-1062.

Palmer, F. "Has Compensatory Education Failed? No, Not Yet." Unpublished manuscript, University of New York, Stony Brook, 1975.

Ryan, S. "Overview."In *A Report on Longitudinal Evaluations of Preschool Programs.* Vol. 1. *Longitudinal Evaluation,* edited by S. Ryan. Washington, D.C.: Department of Health, Education, and Welfare, 1974. Publication No. (OHD) 74-24.

Westinghouse Learning Corporation. *The Impact of Head Start: An Evaluation of the Effects of Head Start on Children's Cognitive and Affective Development. Executive Summary.* Ohio University Report to O.E.O., Clearinghouse for Federal Scientific and Technical Information, June 1969.

White, S. "The National Impact Study of Head Start." In *The Disadvantaged Child, Vol. 3,* edited by J. Hellmuth. New York: Brunner/Mazel, 1970.

Wolff, M., and Stein, A. *Factors Influencing the Recruitment of Children into the Head Start Program,* Summer 1965: A Case Study of Six Centers in New York City (Study II). New York: Yeshiva University (The Office of Economic Opportunity, Project No. 141-61), n.d.

Zigler, E. "The Environmental Mystique: Training the Intellect Versus Development of the Whole Child." *Childhood Education* 46 (1970): 402-412.

Zigler, E. "Project Head Start: Success or Failure?" *Learning* 1, no. 7 (1973): 43-47.

Zigler, E. "Has It Really Been Demonstrated That Compensatory Education Is Without Value?" *American Psychologist* 30 (1975): 935-937.

Education: A Family Responsibility

William G. Demmert, Jr., *Deputy Commissioner, Office of Indian Education, Department of Health, Education, and Welfare, Office of Education, Washington, D.C.*

My presentation will focus on an educational process in the midst of a revolution; a multifaceted system undergoing the stress and strain of major philosophical, administrative, and academic changes; a process that has its roots in local communities with primary support from parents whose children are of school age; a revolution which, if successful, will set the stage for a major reevaluation of contemporary thought about how to solve the problems in American education.

My immediate and direct concern is to improve educational quality and opportunity for Indian children, ensuring their "... safe passage... into adulthood and the citizen's estate" (National Panel on High School and Adolescent Education 1974, p. 38). Indirectly and philosophically this concern applies to all children.

My focus on Indian education allows me to analyze a fairly homogenous set of problems and provide solutions that are not clouded with intercultural variables, which might complicate matters and lead to concentration on peripheral rather than root issues. Indian education is very selective, narrow in scope, and complex. I've spent both my student life and my professional life learning, working, analyzing, and searching for answers in this arena. Indian education is a topic in

17

which I have substantial interest and practical experience and about which I have many biases. I also believe there is substantial opportunity to transfer what we know about Indian education to education in general, and that is what I would like to talk about.

The logical place to begin talking about Indian education is with the definition. It is here that the first problem is encountered. The way in which one defines Indian education depends on the perspective used to get the definition—that is, whether the concepts of the Indian community or the non-Indian community are used. One must distinguish between the "outside" and "inside" definition of Indian education. Historically the "inside," or Indian, definition involved a core curriculum consisting of three subjects: survival, religion, and how to act. These were not mutually exclusive, but were inseparable.* The "outside," or non-Indian, definition depends upon the historical period studied and has fluctuated between extinction (or surrender of cultural identity) and self-determination.

In the late sixties and early seventies, much data was collected on educational achievement among Indians. The average educational level for all Indians was found to be 8.4 years; from grades eight through twelve the dropout rate was estimated variously to be from 39 to 48 percent. Studies showed Indian students scored significantly lower in measures of achievement at every grade than the average White pupil. Compounding this was the finding that the degree of lag was greater at grade twelve than grade one, indicating the longer the Indian student stayed in school the further behind he fell. Twenty-five percent of all Indian children who start school are unable to speak English, demonstrating a vital need for bilingual education. In 1970 a survey showed 36 percent of parents of Indian children had not continued beyond grade school. Parental participation in their children's educational process had been minimal. In 40 percent of the cases surveyed, no teacher-parent interaction relative to pupil progress occurred, and nearly 70 percent of the parents had no contact with teachers regarding their child's behavior.

In addition to the academic problems, we've been told Indian students possess unique and specialized educational needs because of their heritage. Rural isolation, urban assimilation, termination of tribal governments, cultural differences and stereotypes, and the desire to retain an Indian identity are a few contributing factors that directly affect the learning process of our people. Couple this with a diverse multicultural nation and we have educational problems so

---

*Myron Jones, Director, Indian Leadership Training, Inc.: personal communication.

complex that it has taken considerable and continued analysis to identify what is meant by meeting the special educational needs of Indian students. The educational systems Indian children attend—the public school system, the BIA system, and alternative schools—are just beginning to recognize and sensitize themselves to these special needs and deal with them effectively.

In 1972, the Indian Education Act was established as law. What has been accomplished since this time?

1. A positive communication link has been established between the schools serving Indians and the parents of Indian children.

2. An awareness has been stimulated in school districts and State Departments of Education that they have Indian students and there are special educational problems to be solved.

3. A large number of jobs have been created for Indians in local communities, resulting in both a stimulation of the economy and a need for professional training.

4. The Indians' attitude toward schools and schooling has improved. We have seen decreased dropout rates, improvement in attendance rates, and positive attitudinal changes by both school system personnel and the Indian community.

5. Parental interest in the educational process and the progress of their children has resurfaced.

6. A national concern for the educational needs of Indians has risen, with a complete change of attitude and policy by the federal government from one of grudgingly meeting a burden to one of actively and positively meeting a responsibility.

7. Finally, we are experiencing one of the greatest on-the-job training efforts ever implemented in the Indian community through our field reading activities, parent committee and school district interaction, and the administration of Indian projects and programs by Indians. These changes are resulting in the development of the

capacity of Indian communities to significantly
impact the education of their children.

As we continue to improve and expand upon this development,
we must prepare for evaluating its effect in academic achievement
concomitant to efforts made for improving the quality of education for
Indians.

I see two objectives for the Office of Indian Education in helping
to meet the goal of improving the quality of education for Indians: to
help create positive affective changes and positive cognitive changes
on the part of Indian students. The challenge is staggering and can
only be achieved with improved community-school relations, improved student attitudes about school and school attitudes about students, and providing the Indian community an opportunity to impact
the education of their children.

I'd also like to talk about a way of looking at Indian education as
viewed from another perspective. It's personal, and it offers some
insight into my psyche (if you're interested).

My educational process began soon after I was born. Learning
was very informal at first and focused on feeding, physical comfort,
and exercising my vocal cords. Learning soon became formal, culturally biased, and exciting, as the things to learn confronted me faster
than I could learn them. This process was stimulated by the enthusiasm and attention of my parents, grandparents, and relatives.
The memories of this early period are good. I remember sitting on my
grandmother's knee listening to her singing in Tlingit; learning to
dance with certain kinds of movement that told stories about my an-
cestors; that I was Tlingit of the Eagle clan (I later learned that I was
also Oglala Sioux); and that certain things were expected of me. There
were many opportunities to observe my parents and uncles carrying
out their roles in life. I soon became bold enought to first imitate, and
then actually participate in, these activities. I remember picking sea
gull eggs; freezing my feet and hands at night when my folks were
digging clams and cockels; crying when we were picking seaweed at
Warren Island and the waves kept washing the skiff off the beach;
landing the ship at the docks and holding the wheel when traveling
from one village to another over the water; rowing the skiff; picking
berries; gathering and packing wood for the house and smokehouse;
riding a bike; falling through the ice; tipping over a rowboat and re-
gaining consciousness in bed; and other things that helped prepare
me for life in Southeastern Alaska. I also remember when my formal
schooling began—I remember learning to count to 100; taking cod-
liver oil; playing games on the school grounds; picnics after the

school year ended; having trouble spelling; difficult times memorizing arithmetic tables; loving to read comics; listening to stories that were much different than the ones I had heard when listening to my grandparents and their friends talk during the evenings at home while eating soapberries, blueberries, huckleberries, or salmonberries gathered during the summer. I also recall my teacher telling the nurse that I might have excellent hearing but that I sure did not listen very well. I remember preferring to go to my smarter friends when I was having problems with my spelling, English, and other school work for an explanation or help rather than to the teachers. At the same time, I remember working with my dad and uncles on the fishing gear and boat; hunting for seal and deer; digging for red snapper; and picking gumboots. This, too, was an educational process.

During this period of learning, I was told we should be kind to the children that were not Tlingit because they were visitors, that they were not as strong, and that their parents were here to provide services that we did not provide for ourselves. I remember, too, learning that their parents did not make good fishermen, and we should share our catch with them.

These are reflections of my educational process. Regardless of whether these reflections are accurate, distorted, or fantasy, they underline an important point for Indian education. Jerome Bruner once stressed that the educational process passes on and directs the culture of those who control it.* He also emphasized that "the issue [of education] is one of man's capacity for creating a culture, society, and technology that not only feed him but keep him caring and belonging" (Bruner 1971, p. 21). Both of these concepts have substantial implication for Native Americans and their educational process. They also have implications for the public educational system of the nation.

In the Tlingit culture in which I grew up, it was traditional for maternal uncles to formally educate the young men. This formal process began when a child learned to walk, usually with a daily bath in the ocean to toughen him mentally and physically. Other skills necessary to living in the environment were introduced in a timely manner and learned well.

One either learned or perished.

The uncles knew the importance of knowledge and skills and would not accept failure. They had both the authority and responsibility to prepare the young men for the world they lived in. The process

---

*Jerome Bruner, Harvard University, 1971: personal communication.

was formal, yet very flexible. The spring and summer months were spent outside with on-the-job training. The winter months were used for history, improving and participating in cultural activities that were important to growth or further development. Things of importance were reinforced, and things no longer of use became part of the past. Learning was an internal and an integrated part of community life.

This is no longer true in the Tlingit community or in America. The formal education process is too far removed from the family, from the pulse of the community, and is dominated by external forces and interests. The impact of this change has been devastating in the Indian community, and I believe in society in general. We need a marriage of the two: a combination and coordination that provides the family a meaningful role, but a process that brings in experts in areas outside of the family's experience for expanding knowledge and expertise. An outside force brought in for what they have to offer, not because they're part of a system, but because of their skills. Move outside that, and we just play a role. Go through superficial motions, and we find a system that is not doing the job in today's technical world.

Our focus must concentrate on identifying goals, analyzing options for reaching those goals, developing and implementing activities that enable us to succeed in reaching those goals, then evaluating those efforts for redirection or establishment of new goals.

What does this all mean?

1. It means educational reform at its highest level, a reassertion of control and responsibility by parents.

2. It means concentration on activities and processes with evidence of effectiveness, a major focus on quality and appropriateness.

3. It means development of an evaluation system that provides feedback for analysis and redirection when necessary; and finally

4. It means establishment of an educational base for building and stimulating a student's highest potential.

What are some of the goals in the Indian community?

1. Retain an Indian identity and culture using tribalism as the base from which that identity stems.

2. Create a climate that will offer Indian communities an opportunity to refine their cultural development (this means looking into the past, present, and future).

3. Provide the skills necessary to enable Indian children to actively participate and contribute to all arenas of today's world.

In meeting these goals, we can start with the following facts as a basis: (1) The educational process is the conduit for passing on and controlling the culture of our young. (2) The issue of education is one of creating a culture, society, and technology that not only feeds people, but keeps them caring and provides a sense of belonging. (3) A child's early years are critically important to success later in life because cultural, emotional, physical, intellectual, and language abilities are determined or substantially impacted during this period. (4) Self-determination is important to one's well-being and success.

What does all of this have to do with "Education: A Family Responsibility"? I believe that parents are the key to opening the doors of educational success, for Indians as well as for all other cultures:

- They must establish a firm educational base in their newborn for professionals to build upon.

- They must monitor and direct the professional to ensure a process that is compatible to the culture of their children's heritage.

- They must stimulate local, state, and national governments to allow for cultural differences and to provide equal educational opportunities for all children.

- They must take the time to ensure "the safe passage of [their children] into adulthood and the citizen's estate" (National Panel on High School and Adolescent Education 1974, p. 38).

As professionals, we sometimes resent the intrusion of non-professionals in our chosen occupation. We think of it as tampering. If we did not have pride in our own capabilities and expertise, we could not establish a successful system. The problem is that these feelings sometimes overshadow the reason for our existence—the formal education of children and youth. As professionals, we are subjectively involved with educational periphery and objectively involved in educating children. Parents, however, are subjectively interested in their children's welfare and future and are, therefore, in my judgment, the key to education success. Parents will not allow their children to die on the vine.

I think we have reached a point of decay—protection of mediocrity rather than reward for excellence. We are in a period of misdirection similar to one that caused deterioration in corporations, eventually bringing railroads and other giants to their knees. These periods of decay are characterized by activities or decisions that protect the system and are antithetical to the reasons for its existence—in this case, the safe passage of children into adulthood and today's world. Safe passage should provide the proper tools for creating a culture, society, and technology that keep one caring and belonging in the society.

We must look to the past to ensure proper passage of the skills and the educational processes which are still relevant to today.

We must look around us, learn new skills, develop new knowledge so that we can survive and retain our heritage.

We must look beyond our immediate community, those around us, and look at corollaries in other parts of the country and in the world, adjusting and adapting the best for use in our communities and expanding on ideas for new and innovative thrusts that are based on sound reasoning and theory.

At four recent national conferences for Title IV, I talked about a revolution—a revolution in Indian education that will have a significant and positive impact on education in general. A revolution where Indian parents are beginning to participate in their children's education. A revolution that is stimulating renewed efforts to improve quality and relevance.

When major problems in Indian education have been resolved, a process for solving educational problems in other circles for other groups will have begun. We share one thing in common—an intense desire to educate our children to live in society without giving up a unique cultural heritage.

Indians are few in number, but when we work together in what we want educationally, we can support issues as a group. We have an opportunity to do something worthwhile, to move from an era of decay, stagnation, and confusion, to an era of educational excellence.

References

Bruner, J. S. "The Progress of Education Revisited." *Phi Delta Kappan* 53, no. 1 (September 1971): 21.

National Panel on High School and Adolescent Education. "The Education of Adolescents, Part I." Summary, Conclusion, and Recommendations of the Report of the National Panel on High School and Adolescent Education, 1974.

Seminars in Parenting Preschoolers

Polly Greenberg, *Director, The Growth Program, Washington, D.C.*

There are many kinds of parent education, of course, but one approach, which can be used in conjunction with other approaches or as a whole program in and of itself, is seminars in parenting: group discussions, stimulated and guided by a leader on the topic of childraising.

Four to sixteen two-hour sessions in the evening, or at a time convenient for parents, at one week intervals, seem to work well. Many people do not want to meet more than once a week. They don't want to major in parenting. They just want to get some things off their chests or get help in solving a specific problem or meet other parents with whom to talk things over. We parent ed types may want to spend a lifetime at it, but most parents don't. Whatever their walk of life, they have other things to do, and one evening or morning or afternoon a week is all they'll come. (There are exceptions to everything.)

The reason to limit each session to two hours is that that's about the right amount of time to get going, get into it, and get out before boredom sets in—in fact, while interest is still high, and a sense of "there's lots more still to say" brings folks eagerly back next time. Skilled group leaders can successfully pull off longer sessions, but for the average group, two hours is long enough. Why limit each course to four to sixteen classes (depending upon the situation)? Because doing so encourages group leaders to quickly pull concerns and interests from participants and to develop a deep, rich discussion around each emerging subject. If group leaders feel they have eternity ahead of them, they spread material thin to stretch it. Watery gruel never tastes good. On the other hand, if leaders feel they have very little time to accomplish everything, they tend to make each segment of each session count. Though efficiency may work against one objective of some staff members, which might be to prolong a course as long as possible to preserve jobs, nonetheless, efficiency, cost effectiveness, and intensive quality continue to be the goal of some program planners. One way to achieve quality in a program is to structure the situation to bring out the best in group leaders.

Yet even though the program is designed to dodge the most insidious Parkinsonian problem bureaucratic programs traditionally have (that is, that work expands to fill the time allotted to it), it's counterproductive to plan a lot, develop curriculum, develop agendas, and develop anxiety, if group leaders are good *discussion* leaders. Discussion is considerably inhibited by the constant intrusion of next items on the agenda. When the leader senses the logical, natural flow of the evolving discussion, he or she should be free to move with it, not be hog tied by a prefabricated sequential outline. The sequence should be furnished by "on site" parent concerns, not by absentee theoreticians.

Groups with between seven to fifteen members work best for discussion. When there are more than fifteen people, all of whom come ripe with needs, some individuals have to wait so long for their "case" to be heard, that they become disgruntled or drop out altogether. It must be remembered that seminars in parenting are not straight adult education courses to which people come to passively receive information through their ears alone. They come to seek *personal* information, alternatives, to solve problems, to be reassured as *individual* parents by people who've heard their situation. Remaining anonymous in the group for a whole session is not compatible with the need that brought them forth from their homes. Of course a clever leader could give each person in a group larger than fifteen a chance to speak, but there wouldn't be time to study a case in depth, to delve for details, to develop a clear picture of the context, interpersonal and otherwise, surrounding the circumstance being presented by the parent, therefore to give help. When fewer than seven are present, it turns into a counseling session. Parenting seminars should not be one-to-one psychological counseling or anything closely resembling it.

For our purposes, who is a good discussion leader?

A good discussion leader has, or can quickly earn, the respect of the group. Respect will not come via mere credentials, though these may render the group silent due to intimidation and expectation that "**the answer**" is forthcoming. Respect is earned through facilitating something seen as useful by parents, and by making them feel they have great potential as developing parents, not by making them feel the experts disapprove of them.

Probably the most likely candidates to succeed at this kind of group leading are:

- Child development specialists with good interpersonal skills who are skilled at the art of leading discussion and who are "creative coper" type parents.

- Persons otherwise relevantly professionally qualified (psychiatric social work, affective education, etc.) who are interpersonally skilled, skilled at the art of leading discussion, who are "creative coper" type parents, and who have been given a short course in the *content* of seminars in parenting (child development and family dynamics).

If neither of the above is available, the successful parent, generally respected by parents in his/her community, with good interpersonal skills, can sometimes be trained in child development and in discussion guiding skills. Not always. This person may have too superficial a knowledge of personality and interpersonal dynamics to help parents dig to the root of the matter, or too contrived or insensitive an approach to the delicate art and science of discussion leading.

Another possible candidate for the position of parent seminar discussion leader is the person who is good in child development and seminar work but who isn't a parent. (Then pray nobody challenges them on playing parenting expert when they ain't even a one-time parent.)

A good discussion leader can *promptly* begin to pull "real live" concerns from participants. Beginning with gimmicks, games, or canned curriculum is beginning circuitously (in the former instance), remotely and abstractly (in the latter). Though there's no harm in it, it's a waste of time compared to zeroing in to the core of it all: specific situations specific parents are faced with from which specific, pivotal principles of personality development can be pulled and more generally applied.

Asking each participant to write on a name tag the name he or she wished to be called and the names and ages of the children is a good activity to engage in while the group gathers. Refreshments that people have to get up and get at this time are also a helpful mixer relaxer. "If you have a specific problem or topic you want to be sure we discuss during these sessions, please write it on this slip of paper so we can be sure not to miss it." Make it clear that this is not a guarantee to talk about it today, but a promise to take it up as thoroughly as is desired during the "course."

As soon as everyone has assembled and the leader has spent ten or fifteen minutes in casual social conversation with individuals or small clusters of people, he or she can start out by smilingly inquiring if anyone has anything in mind to kick off with. Wait, smile, look, listen, don't be afraid of silence. If no one speaks after a few minutes (which rarely happens!), we can say laughingly, "Well, great, let's have another cup of coffee and go home. What a wonderful group, no one has a single problem raising perfect children! Teach *me* how, will you?—I myself have some trouble raising *my* kids." This infallibly gets the ball rolling. It establishes an informal, friendly atmosphere. It announces that the group leader is (a) a parent and (b) human. As a last resort, if no one contributes a start up topic, the leader could say, "Well, let's see, let's pick a slip of paper at random here and just get to work wherever we want to."

A good discussion leader is good at pacing; can speed things up if a lag is lurking around the next paragraph spoken; can stop the onward flow of the discussion and channel it downward toward depth and valuable information, ideas, etc., lying beneath the current waiting only to be towed up where they can be examined; can get a new topic started on the heels of the completion of the last one if the latter "feels" finished.

A good discussion leader avoids answering questions, but never avoids facing issues and giving help. To answer a question is to give a person a fish. To guide the person, with the group's assistance, to *multiple alternative solutions to the problem* is to teach that person, *and the group, how* to fish. Though most parents, like most students, try to get "teacher" to answer the question head-on, it remains true that teaching the process is giving a lifelong skill, whereas giving the answer is supplying only momentary relief from the struggle presented by living. In teaching parenting as in teaching mathematics, telling an individual "243" isn't anywhere near as useful as going carefully through the process of arriving at 243 with the whole group so everyone ends up *understanding* how to do long division.

Amateur or inadequate discussion leaders want tight curriculums because they fear they won't know the answer. Ph.D.s in child development may have this uneasiness as well as nontrained people. In fact, the more research-oriented group leaders are, the more they tend toward caution. Parents aren't seeking the absolute truth as yet to be defined by science through thousands of incontrovertably "true" precision research studies. They seek practical help in creatively coping with actual nitty-gritty realities confronting them. Therefore, a creative, confident parent with training in the art of discussion leading often makes a better group leader for our purposes than does a more rigid type personality with scads of child development courses and scores of academic-type brownie points.

A good discussion leader for a seminar for parents on parenting encourages people to come up above the trees that stymie them, and to examine the forest. In other words, regardless of what subtopic is being talked about (toilet training, table manners, toy picking up, or whatever), we pull and stretch it toward, "Well, but, how can we *know* if we're handling it the best way until we think about our objectives and goals?" For example, if the objective of childraising is only a clean baby, we can beat the child every time for failure to use the bathroom correctly. But if the objective *is also* to develop a kind, empathetic person, perhaps we should bathroom train the child through methods that are *kind and empathetic.* And so on, no matter what subject is the subject of discussion. We help parents take a look at what they believe in, what kind of human beings they're attempting to develop, and to locate methods of childraising likely to produce desired results. A constant question to ask parents is, "Is what so-and-so just said consistent with the idea you all told me you want, developing an honest (or whatever) child?"

A good discussion leader can draw out the silent few that sit on the sidelines of all groups or can at least converse with them apart from the others to ascertain that their silent observation is volitional or to determine with them means of making it easier for them to talk. Some people's concerns are being brought out by others. Some people learn better by listening. It tickles our vanity to see people talk as the result of our discussion guiding, but some people have no need to speak to get what they want from the group. However, it's the group leader's responsibility to check this out with nontalkers in case they are frustrated and do wish to join in. Equally as important as bringing in the "fringer," is hushing up the "monopolizer" or tactfully handling the "tangenter" and graciously getting back on the track of a rich vein of exploration or a hot issue in terms of the group's interest.

A good leader of discussion on this particular subject—parenting—is a skillful *affective* adult educator. There is a difference between adult education of an informational nature, such as agriculture, and adult education that deals with feelings, conflicts, and the problems faced by all human beings in the most vulnerable aspect of their lives, the personal, domestic aspect. Though there is much information to be shared, there's a lot more to trying new approaches on timeworn problems than just information. Information on child development fills innumerable books and magazines in every library. If information alone were all that was needed, every parent in the nation would do better if we gave him or her a library card.

There are several pitfalls in the paths of ingenue group leaders. The first is the danger of giving a well-prepared lecture-style course in child development, which lays forth before the politely listening parents how the child develops and unfolds from birth to adolescense. This fails to help most parents. To be effective in assisting people toward improved childraising, parenting seminars should be *affective* education—education of the feelings, as well as of the mind. There never has been a parent yet who raised a child through intellect alone. In the first place, parents repeat in their childraising practices the way they were raised, or rebel against some or all elements of it. It's necessary, if helping a parent change *behavior* which is causing a problem in the child or in the family is an objective, to listen to the parent describe what he or she feels the child is not doing right, encourage each parent in the group to describe what he or she does in relation to the disquieting factor, and then to find out how the *parents'* parents handled *them* or felt about this area with *them* when they were children. People need to gain some degree of emotional understanding of the dynamics of what's going on if they are to get control of their behavior, *choose* an alternative, and *act differently.*

In the second place, parents act in relation to their needs and the needs of other family members, not just in vacuous response to knowledge of abstract child development. Consequently, to help a *parent* is to help a parent see personal needs and family needs, as well as the needs of the particular child being discussed, and fitting it all together. The only way to do this is to pull from the parent all the particulars of the whole scene—the parent is the only one present who has these facts.

The hard part of helping parents is:

- To help parents see that a problem exists in terms of satisfactorily resolving the troublesome situation or in terms of parenting consistently with their own childraising objectives.
- To help parents discover alternatives to their way of handling the problem.

- To help parents feel that there is no *right* way, but there are more and less effective ways, and there are ways more or less consistent with the development and maintenance of sound mental health for all concerned.

- To help parents feel free to experiment and revert to the familiar way if no favorable results occur in a few weeks or months time.

- To help parents feel power in their ability to positively effect their child—the "environment" must be pinpointed and made less mysterious and overwhelming—the environment is essentially *parents,* especially in the instance of young children.

- To help parents feel accountable for applying what they believe to the task of developing a human being—the experts aren't raising this child, the individual parent is.

Parent education is *affective* education. It deals with psychological and interpersonal facts, with ethnic and sociometric facts, not only with information. Therefore, to do this work well, a group leader needs a good deal of sensitivity.

Yet, we are definitely *not* getting into group therapy. The goal is *not* self-revelation, soul-cleansing openness for the sake of nonrepression. The goals are aiding parents in solving or at least alleviating specific major or minor problems they are experiencing in raising their children; to help them develop greater awareness of the psycho-social dynamics that apply to us all; and to help them feel better about themselves as parents.

Due to the nature of the feelings and material we work with, we must be fully capable of keeping confidential information confidential. Confidentiality requires that a group leader repeat nothing personal outside the group. It also demands that the leader remind the group, after a sensitive session, that we must all honor each other's privacy and keep what we know of other people's problems to ourselves.

Often, only one parent (of a pair) wishes to attend, because a key part of the childraising problem is disagreement with the other parent in the partnership. Confidentiality here may mean providing an opportunity for the parent seeking to solve the problem to learn alternatives, to gain strength, and to create strategies for coping with the absent parent. Insisting that both parents attend the parent seminar is by no means always wise. It's better to help one parent grow in problem-solving and childraising skills than to insist so much on the presence of both that neither comes. Sometimes what the parent who comes needs is referral to an appropriate agency or person to aid the other parent (alcoholic counseling, a pastor, a mental health center, etc.) or to aid the partnership (marriage counseling). If often happens that a parent seminar serves as a readiness class for really tackling a family problem. Also, many times one parent is simply more interested in "studying" childraising than the other, just as one parent might want to take an English literature course, and the other wouldn't. It isn't essential to have both parents present in order to help their children.

Due to the sensitivity of the subject area, it's vital that group leaders be warmly supportive. A complicated question that often arises is: How can you be warmly supportive of a parent who is doing something appalling?

Number one, the leader can comment with pleasure on the fact that the parent brought this up in the group. "I'm *so* glad you brought that up, Barbara; I'm sure many people here have something somewhat like that on their minds." Such a statement praises the fact that the parent provided a diving board for discussion, not that she locked her child in the closet for three hours.

Secondly, after listening nonjudgmentally, asking further questions about what, why, etc., ask the parents if this method of handling the situation is consistent with the development of characteristics they have earlier listed as those they seek to inculcate in their offspring: affection, honesty, cooperation, etc. Confronting individuals with a sharp discrepancy between what they do and what they allege they are trying to achieve is a very effective way of causing *thinking.* In some cases, thinking precedes behavioral change. This isn't always true.

Thirdly, ask if anyone in the group can think of other ways such a situation might be handled. Collect suggestions, each time focusing on whether or not the suggestion (a) seems likely to be effective, (b) seems consistent with the long-term development of sound mental health, and (c) seems practical to the parent who originated the discussion. If the parent resists the less alarming way of handling whatever the situation was, we can point out that some things which "work" in the present lead to behavioral boomerangs or personality damage in the future.

Here it's useful to make a joke, and ask, "Who's willing to do some homework? Let's assign 'the skill of the week.' Everybody go home and practice doing thus and such" (a skill suitable to the situation under discussion) "and when we come back next week, tell us how it worked. Probably some of you already *use* this particular parenting skill. Will you be good enough to watch yourself and look for examples of how and when you do it and what happens when you do? Will you? I hope you will, it'll be a big help to all of us. And you, Barbara, will you try it and see what you think of it?" Enlist everyone's help. Most people are pleased to find themselves in helping roles.

At this point, it's often useful to say, "I have a book here which makes some interesting points on this subject. You might want to take it home and look it over. You may not agree with the author, but it never hurts to think about something from a different perspective." Put the book in the person's hand, point out the pertinent chapter, and conclude the conversation with, "If you find anything in there you think would interest the group will you tell us next week?" You are showing confidence in the parent's judgment. Parents will respect you for this.

It's helpful to carry a carton of suitable books to each class. Books selected should meet these criteria:

- They should be lively, interesting reading rather than lugubrious "more-than-I-care-to-know" texts full of jargon and theories.
- They should deal with the business of *raising* children and living in families, the interaction of parents and children, not with the history of child development or child development theory.
- There should be one or more on each specialty subject one may find in any group: divorce, single parenting, an alcoholic in the family, a death in the family, and so on.
- There should be some on education: day care, preschool, and all the other levels of education.
- There should be *many* titles by authors of various persuasions.

If *one* book is used, it promotes the erroneous idea that experts have answers, or *think* they do, and that all parents have to do is apply the answers to the child, like a coat of paint to the wall. With many books, parents will get two messages (which the group leader can mention more than once):

35

- All specialists related to child development, human development, personality psychiatry or psychology, early childhood education, family living, pediatrics, and so on, *agree on many basic principles of developmental mental health.* These "scientific facts" we may want to think about seriously.

- Each specialist who writes a book has some different slant, emphasis, technique, or point to make. If this were not the case, no publisher would invest the thousands of dollars necessary to get the book published. One parent or another may find one idea or another *excellently helpful in his or her situation.*

   To maximize the value of recommending readings for parents, it's imperative that the leader suggest a book with a needed slant for each person. For instance, some parents see themselves as doormats for their children to stamp and trample upon. Avoid giving these parents books urging parents to let their children make decisions. Strive to give such parents books insisting upon the rights of mothers, parents, and other people besides the child. Other parents constantly feel guilty. They harangue themselves half to death about the rightness and dangers of every childraising detail. Give them books which are very reassuring; which stress the point that if parents provide the foundation triangle of love, limits, and independence, the rest will evolve naturally, and children will grow up to be O.K. adults without a lot of hassle. Controlling parents (the leader, and for that matter the entire group, will promptly spot these people) should be given books which urge "the child is a person, allow him leeway, let her make decisions, give her some life-space in which you don't encroach." Etc.

   The reason to hand out books rather than bibliographies is self-evident. Few people have the motivation or time to go to a library or bookstore. The library may not own the book, or it may be out. Bookstores never have the book you're looking for; bookstores are obsolete. By the time the person and the book get together, the group has long since disbanded. A book in hand makes it possible for a clever group leader to take advantage of a learning opportunity that crops up spontaneously. Some parents don't read. But they hear the authors' ideas as reported upon by group participants, and as expanded upon during sessions by the discussion leader, who may want to clarify or underline key points. Articles and pamphlets can be used in addition to books, *if* they pass the above criteria, which many of them don't. The same is true of brief digests staff do of appropriate books, providing *no major point the author makes is distorted or omitted.* The problem here is that most people, including professionals, can't read very well, so tend to twist the author's intent during the act of digesting.

Anxious future group leaders often ask: "What topics should be taken up?" Here it must be reemphasized that if an "open classroom," emerging curriculum approach is relied upon, *participants in parenting seminars will bring up the topics;* group leaders need not stay up until the small wee hours biting their fingernails and worrying if their lists are all-inclusive. What topics? *Any* topics obvious to those familiar with the realities or the literature of young children. A quick glance at the tables of contents of a few books on living with children or operating preschool programs will yield enough curriculum for many, many sessions. For starters, the following leap to mind; doubtless dozens more will pop up while these are being considered:

child's needs	aggression: positive, negative
child doesn't listen	avoiding junk foods when other children eat them
children's fears	
children's feelings	clinging, dependent children
daily stress	communication
fantasy/reality	day care or not, and what kind
finicky eaters	cooperation: how much? when?
handling frustration	disagreement between parents
how children learn	
lying/stealing	discipline: constructive? punishment?
mother's responsibilities	independence: how much? when?
obese children	motor skill development: large, small
parent's feelings	nursery school or not, and what kind
parent's needs	obedience: how much? when?
parent's guilt	situational distrubances (moving)
raising the urban child	special problems in suburbia
sex (information, education, sexuality, stereotypes)	temper tantrums
sibling problems	to work or not to work
the *other* children's needs	toilet training
the *other* parent's needs	young child's need for young friends

Some group leaders worry that participants won't learn about ages and stages this way. With good guidance, they will. But the sequence moves from the ages, stages, and situations that interest each group member first, and then fans out to include ages, stages, and situations already in the past, and ages, stages, and situations yet to come. The parent whose two-year-old is biting, flailing, hitting, and wailing will be nothing but annoyed if we sit there solemnly weighing breast or bottle. The difference is that traditional education starts with the interests of curriculum specialists and hopes to hook the interest of students, while progressive education starts with the burning concerns of the students, and is structured by specialists to evolve as far, wide, and deep as students will go. The idea is, "Your concerns are our curriculum."

Before it's all over, someone invariably asks, "But what about evaluation?" As all of us know, it's always easier to do things as private business, or as a private professional service (lawyers, doctors, and so on) than to do them with public funds. To get public funds you usually first have to prove you're inventing the wheel, even if everybody including yourself knows it was invented years ago and has been reinvented in every state and nation since (parent education is as old as the hills, and there are many old pros around to consult). After you write bulky proposals to prove you're inventing the wheel, which take so much staff time to write that it's hard to locate a few minutes to work with parents, then you have to prove your work worked. To do this, one is expected to create all sorts of scientific-looking contrivances and statistics which will convince fund givers of the significance of this project, and of the fact that clearly it should be heartily refunded.

In the private sector, we are free to evaluate our success or lack of it by such modest commonsense measures as:

- Do parents call, pay, come, participate, and express enthusiasm for what we're doing?

- Do they tell others who call, pay, come, participate, and express enthusiasm for what we're doing?

Of course, if our objective in conducting seminars in parenting is to change parents' childraising practices in all dimensions and permanently, we can toss out the assessment tools and confess right off that we *inevitably,* in *every instance,* fail. However, if the objective is to be one more drop in the bucket in human growth and development for adults—specifically for parents—to add a few alternatives, to insert a few insights, to provide a bit of support and relief, to assist people in the process of reducing the more strenuous and persistent of their childraising problems to slightly more manageable or endurable proportion, then we can trust our eyes, ears, and impressions. However, for those who must come up with formal written evaluation, there is probably little to do other than to repeat the pattern devised decades ago by grantees good at grantsmanship: grind out some forms, gather some irrelevant but important-looking facts, and fake it.

As for the other parent seminarists, we can reassure ourselves by remembering that "help" is defined by those whom do-gooders aim to help. If they appear helped, let us have faith and accept this as positive evaluation of our efforts.

Piaget's Affective System— An Appraisal

E. James Anthony, *Blanche F. Ittleson Professor of Child Psychiatry and Director, Eliot Division of Child Psychiatry, Washington University School of Medicine, St. Louis, Missouri.*

Piaget has had such an overwhelming impact in this country on the education of young children in the area of their cognitive development that his contributions to the understanding of the child's feelings and fantasies have been overlooked. Three possible reasons might account for this:

1. Piaget has considerably underplayed his work in this area.
2. The psychologists who introduced him to the American public have been, for the most part, cognitive psychologists and have treated it with scant attention.
3. The educators have been so impressed by the sudden appearance of a rational, ready-made curriculum based on the operational concept that they have preoccupied themselves with fitting it to the educational system.

It takes a clinician, like myself, who works predominantly with the emotions of children to pick out what amounts to, when put together, a not insubstantial affective subsystem within Piaget's general theory. Furthermore, he treats the subject so covertly and so sporadically that it is quite difficult to isolate from the general body of his work. This relative obscurity

41

is further accentuated by the absence of the many brilliant insights that constantly illuminate his investigation of the intellectual process. There are no haunting phrases that label it immediately a Piagetian approach. One could, in fact, read all thirty volumes describing this psychology and be left in the end with the conviction that the emotional life of the child had been entirely overlooked. In an earlier article (Anthony 1957), I went so far as to caricature Piaget's approach by describing it as a "psychology without emotion," and contrasting it with psychoanalysis as the "psychology without cognition," which was equally untrue. In this presentation, almost twenty years later, some effort will be made to repair this global and somewhat erroneous epithet.

The first question we should ask ourselves is why someone with a good understanding of the total child cut himself short in the area of affect. Piaget (1952) offers some explanation in his autobiography. It was, he said, his mother's emotional instability and its disturbing effect upon him that led him to avoid any dealings with clinical matters and to restrict himself to "the study of normalcy and the workings of the intellect." He recognized, however, that his reaction was an ambivalent one since he also, at the beginning of his studies, felt "intensely interested in questions of psychoanalysis and pathological psychology." His curiosity led him to the Bügholzli Hospital in Zurich where he made the acquaintance of psychiatric cases and formulated his "clinical method" that was later to become his main instrument for the gathering of data.

If one had to write a case history of Piaget (and to a certain extent he has done this himself), one would emphasize the impact of his mother's emotionalism on his early development. As he says, he gave up play, and all the feelings bound up with play, for serious, systematic work beginning in early childhood. He detested any departure from reality and took refuge in "a private and non-fictitious world." He became obsessionally involved in inventions, zoological classifications, and shell collections. He occupied himself endlessly with these studies that were far too serious to be called hobbies, and by the age of ten his first article on an albino sparrow was published in a natural history journal.

However much these intellectual preoccupations helped him to keep his own affects depressed, between the ages of 15 and 20 he experienced a series of emotional crises due to family conditions as well as to the intellectual conflicts of adolescence. Just as he found it hard to reconcile the model presented by his father's scholarly bent with his mother's neurotic temperament, so it seemed equally difficult to synthesize the varying points of view of religion, philosophy, biology, and psychology into a coherent system. Life, at this time, was made up of emotional and intellectual shocks. He began to write down his ideas in numerous notebooks (a habit he has maintained to the present time). He read and wrote prodigiously, leaving no time for any recreational life; as a result he became emotionally upset and was sent up to the mountains for a year to recuperate. It was during this time that he laid the foundation for what was later to become his system.

But affects continued to plague him, and for the rest of his life he has coped with what seemed to be a permanent reservoir of anxiety by filling up all free time with cognitive activity. In this sense, he uses thought to drive out feeling. His life style and his professional bent are therefore consonant in this important respect.

Yet somewhere the vision of a complete human being reflected in the workings of a complete psychological system remains throughout all the vicissitudes of these major defense mechanisms.

The Inseparable Tie

Piaget has persistently maintained from his earliest writings that affect and intelligence were two distinct but complimentary and inseparable aspects of behavior, performing different but essential functions in adapting the individual to the environment, and undergoing a parallel development with corresponding stages. Neither affect nor intelligence, he thought, could be regarded as prior, predominant, or causal with respect to each other. The two components had developed a *modus vivendi* in the operations of everyday life. What remained mysterious and intriguing to Piaget was the reciprocal nature of this relationship. To understand this fully, he would have needed to know more about affect than he did, but time was running out. He had already spent half a century in the pursuit of almost pure reason and to set up a new project of "clinical interrogations" involving the emotions would have demanded at least another fifty years.

It is therefore not surprising that he preferred to take the easier way out and simply state that many of his findings about intelligence could be applied with equal validity to affect, allowing for appropriate modifications. The one system furnished a rough paradigm for the other. Since, however, the affective system did not contain logical structures, it could not aspire to complete equilibrium, the *summmum bonum* of Piaget's system. Nevertheless, the parallelism was close. To quote him:

> I think that in the affective field one would also find the
> equivalent of what logic is in the cognitive field; it would
> be structurations of social concepts in the form of scales
> of moral values. . . .(Tanner and Inhelder 1960)

Such a statement has more heuristic than empirical value and
Piaget is well aware that he has little data to support it. He therefore
goes on to add:

> However, this does not concern me and I will limit myself
> to what I have experience of, that is to the facts of logical
> structures. (Tanner and Inhelder 1960)

Here it was that he felt at home and not as uncomfortable as in
the presence of affects. He goes on to say, perhaps with his tongue in
his cheek (a not unusual posture for Piaget), that he had "not the
slightest desire to generalize from the case of logic to all the rest of
mental life" (Tanner and Inhelder 1960). Yet, this is what he goes on to
do on the basis that affect and cognition are but two sides of the same
coin. This enables him, somewhat spaciously, to present a comprehensive system of psychology with only half of it actually under
construction. The emotional half is exceedingly thin and threadbare.
In truth, affect is the ghost in Piaget's system. It haunts him (and his
readers) throughout the seemingly endless research protocols dealing with the cognitive process, so that one is constantly left wondering
what else the child was up to apart from thinking. Well, we all have a
shrewd suspicion of what children in our experience are up to most of
the time, but it simply does not appear as such in Piaget's protocols.
In his earlier work, written at a time that he humorously refers to as
his protolithic period, there are suggestive "Squeaks from the attic"
that could be understood as the attentuated voice of affect, but these
all disappeared when his interest began to focus more exclusively on
the various manifestations of operational thinking. Thereafter, little is
heard but the sounds of continuous problem solving. At times, he was
driven back into the area of affect whenever the material under investigation transcended its cognitive boundaries, as in the case of play,
dreams, symbolism, or morality (Piaget 1932, 1951).

To paraphrase a well-known quotation about obesity, it seems
to me that in every cognitive system, there seems to be an affective
system struggling to get out. This becomes evident only when cognitions are asked to explain phenomena beyond their capacity. One
authority (Dulit 1972) on Piaget has compared his system to the movie
projector, the running of which is equivalent to the cognitive process,
with the power equated to affect. One is hardly conscious of the role

of the electric current until it fails and only then does one become aware of how essential it is to the total operation.

Piaget never talks about emotions or feelings in any way. He prefers to make use of the French idiom "affectivity" for which there is no real translation since the concept does not exist in English. When questioned about feelings, he tends to evade the issue or change the context. For example, in an illuminating dialogue with Evans, the latter asked him what he thought about the importance of love in the development of the child and Piaget replied in the following way:

> I have no idea about love, but affectivity certainly is central. Affectivity is the motor of any conduct. But affectivity does not modify the cognitive structure. Take two school children for example. One who loves mathematics, who is interested and enthusiastic, and anything else you wish; and the other who has feelings of inferiority, dislikes the teacher, and so forth. One will go much faster than the other, but for both of them two and two make four in the end. It doesn't make three for the one who doesn't like it and five for the one who does. Two and two are still four. (Evans 1973)

He goes on to talk about Janet's (1925) theory of affectivity and the regulation of elementary feeling which is the basis of Piaget's own theory of affectivity. You will notice how quickly he shifted from the personal (dealing with the need for love in early life) to the impersonal concept of affectivity, and that when he used "love," he transposes it into an entirely new key, that is, the love of mathematics, and he continued *as if* he was talking about the same subject as Evans. Exactly what affectivity means to Piaget is difficult to say. To quote Konrad Lorenz: "If an observer like Piaget calls something 'affectivity,' I rely blindly on the assumption that there is a natural unit corresponding to the term. But I find it very difficult to ascertain what exactly that unit is" (Tanner and Inhelder 1960). I must confess that I have the same problem as Lorenz, but would regard "affectivity" as a somewhat desiccated conceptualization of the emotions from which all feelings have been eradicated and reduced to a quasi-cognitive, somewhat logical idea. As defined by Piaget, the concept becomes even more arid:

> I would say that affectivity is the regulation of values, everything which gives a value to the aim, everything which releases interest, effort, etc., and I would say that cognitive functions are the totality of structural regulation. (Tanner and Inhelder 1960)

45

Let me now try and describe the affective portion of Piaget's system. It is not easy to put together as a coherent whole since it is scattered throughout his work in a way that makes it relatively inaccessible.

Piaget's Theory of Affect

To start with, Piaget takes a positive view of affects as they are manifested from the start of life in the baby's almost joyful and zestful exploration of his or her immediate environment. The Piaget baby really appears to be conducting "a love affair with the world," undertaking almost ceaseless experiments on it. Step by step, the child constructs reality, creates environment, and conceptualizes objects, and the whole process is saturated with excitement, curiosity, surprise, and delight. This portrait of active commerce with the world is the hallmark of Piaget's outlook, and it is essentially a composite of cognition and affect from which all negative feelings (anxiety, depression, guilt, shame, etc.) are completely missing.

The model is an epigenetic one in every respect, presupposing a constant interaction between maturational and environmental forces and a constant interaction between the individual and the external world. The differentiation of self from nonself and the changing structure of each is mutually derived from this continuing dialectic. The motivation behind all this activity is not material reward, as might be assumed in an "M & M economy," but the sheer pleasure of doing and getting done. To use Buhler's expression it is a *Funktionslust*.

Let me try and summarize Piaget's affect system in general terms before dealing with it in particular. Here are the main points about it:

1. It is an interactional system in which affects reach out to the environment and accompany practical and reflective intellectual activity. If to think is to be operational, to feel is also to be operational. The affects energize the total process.

2. Like the cognitive system, affects are served by the invariant functions of assimilation and accomodation striving toward equilibrium but never, in this instance, achieving it. The incoming environmental data are taken in and modified by the individual's current affective structure.

3. This current affective structure has been gradually built up through affective experiences from the beginning of life and undergoes ceaseless alteration with the changing demands of development.

4. At a certain stage, consciousness enters the picture and allows for the development of autonomy, socialized behavior, and self-awareness. With the resolution of egocentrism, the child begins to differentiate between his or her own affects and the affects of others.

Affective Development

Piaget has consistently insisted that intelligence and affectivity undergo interrelated and parallel developments (Piaget 1932, 1953, 1973). From birth onward, the infant is subjected to alternating states of pleasure and unpleasure but gradually comes to link two sources in the environment. As the infant's concept of objects is refined, his attitude toward them becomes graduated into positive or negative affective responses that are associated with positive or negative affective structures within him. Because they are more important sources of satisfaction and distress than inanimate objects, human beings are especially liable to have strong positive or negative values attached to them. In fact, the first object in the infant's life to be endowed with permanence is the human object.

During the early period of sensorimotor development, affects are very much intraindividual and presocial. The repertoire is limited to elementary emotions and sentiments that undergo a primitive type of regulation. These elementary affects are generated by perceptions, pain, and pleasure, and secondary reactions related to effort and its success or failure.

With the development of language and other symbolic capacities, the affects gradually become socialized and interindividual. The child makes use of intuitive affects of sympathy and antipathy and becomes able to understand the affects of others, differentiating these from his own. The first moral feelings appear at this time, connected to beliefs and prohibitions stemming from the parents. (In his earlier days, when he was still very much influenced by psychoanalysis, Piaget was inclined to ascribe phenomena such as artificialism to urinary and anal fantasies. The feelings of guilt and punishment associated with masturbation were due, he said, to a systematic fear of retribution residing in things, which he termed "immanent justice.") These ideas of guilt and punishment originate in the constraints imposed by the adult on the child who eventually projects these ideas onto everything. In one of Piaget's early memories, he would go looking for animals to add to his natural history collection. On days when he had anything at all to reproach himself with, he had the strong feeling that he would find very little because of his misdeeds.

A distinct change in the affect system occurs during the period of concrete operations. More equilibrium becomes possible at this time, and Piaget has wondered to what extent the psychoanalytic concept of an effective latency is a function of the equilibration process (Tanner and Inhelder 1960). The child can now form groupings of values and grade them according to their relative priorities. He can also postpone affects in accordance with future needs as a result of the ability to "decenter," and this brings more of his behavior under the control of the will. Morality also undergoes changes as the child comes under the increasing influence of both the peer group and inner autonomy. Games are played according to flexible conventions that are drawn up and decided upon by the players. Morality is altogether less primitive, less exacting, and more in keeping with the principle of mutual respect between equals.

At the onset of the formal stage, feelings become increasingly "decentered" and values and motives are based on sentiments attached to collective ideas and ideals. Intellectual capacity is now on a par with the adult so that angry, resentful, and rebellious feelings can be channeled into constructive criticisms based on sound propositional thinking.

Affective Structures

Running in parallel with the outward manifestations of the development of affect is an inner mental structure that gradually gets built up starting from elementary schemas laid down at the beginning of life. Since affective life, like cognitive life, is part of the total adaptation of the individual to the environment, it shares in the following processes and structures:

1. Reciprocal, recognitory, reproductive, and generalizing assimilations.
2. Resulting from this, the construction of affective schemas similar to cognitive schemas and rep-

resenting relatively stable modes of feeling and reacting.

3. As a result of these assimilations and schematic constructions, there is a continuous accomodation to the current external situation.

4. As with cognition, equilibration is continuous between affective assimilation and accomodation.

5. As a result of this movement toward equilibrium, a conscious regulation of feelings, values, and sentiments takes place under the direction of the will. If, however, there is a primacy of assimilation over accomodation, unconscious symbolic activity begins to take place.

6. Roughly, preoperational affects correspond to preoperational cognitions with similar schema systems, and operational affects are comparable to operational cognitions. In comparison with intellectual schemas, affective schemas seem generally to remain more unconscious, possibly because they are exposed to less accomodation and it is also true that the assimilation of affects takes place with less awareness than cognitive assimilations. In fact, the only way in which one becomes aware of affective assimilations is through the medium of symbolic activity.

The early personal schemas hold closely to the principles of assimilation and the cognitive and affective components are always equally manifest in them. It is only later that intelligence and affect show predominances. In fact, schemas are always compounded as cognitive-affective structures, though one or the other may be salient. As Piaget puts it (in an unusual use of everyday human speech): "We do not love without seeking to understand, and we do not even hate without a subtle use of judgment" (Piaget 1951).

The Language of Affect

According to Piaget, the language of affect has the following characteristics:

1. It is independent of verbal signs.

2. It contains two sets of symbols, metaphors (that are conscious) and cryptophors (that are unconscious).

3. It is used almost exclusively in dreams, daydreams, symbolic activity, and play.

4. It is idiosyncratic, autistic, and mainly rooted in the unconscious.

The child speaks this kind of affective language when under internal pressure with a need to satisfy ego demands on the one side and an affective purpose on the other. According to Piaget affectivity and symbolism are very closely connected: the more intense the affect, the more frequent are the secondary or symbolic assimilations. The cryptophors are different from the usual play symbols in that they are more directly related to the child's ego and involve relatively permanent affective schemas.

Dreams represent another form of affective language and appear to be a continuation of symbolic play both in its primary and secondary varieties. One of Piaget's surprising findings was the close similarity between the content of dreams and play at the corresponding developmental levels. In contrast to the waking, operational world, affects are predominant in dreams while the cognitive processes are vague and uncertain.

Affective Content

The content associated with affect is most vivid in preoperational or nonoperational activities such as symbolic play, dreams, and fantasies. It is in dealing with this that Piaget shows himself to be clinically sensitive. He classifies the affective content expressed by preschool children into three groups: the first relating to eating and excreting activities; the second, to love and hate relationships within the family; and the third to birth anxieties. He points out that these categories are similar to those found in patients undergoing psychoanalysis. Unconscious or secondary symbolism reveals its presence by certain affective signals such as undue excitement and embarrassment (Piaget 1951).

The following vignettes (Piaget 1951) remind us once again of his immense empathy with regard to the cognitive-affective processes in small children.

1. *On Masculine Protest*
   Girl (5.8) "Why do boys need a long thing for that? They could do it through their navel."

2. *On Birth Fantasies*
   Girl (3.9) When someone was arguing with her, she said: "No, don't do that. You know I have a little baby inside me and it hurts him. You know, when my little baby is born, he'll kick you and knock you down." She said to her father: "I want to go back inside you, and then when I come out, I'll be a little baby again. I'll be called Y (the masculine form of her name) because I'll be a boy." (5.9) She played at being in bed for a confinement, declaring that a certain doll was hers, "because it came out of my inside."

3. *On Ambivalence Toward Parent Figures*
   Girl (5.3) Enlisted one of her imaginary companions to cut off her father's head as a means of avenging her at a time when she was on bad terms with him. "But she had some very strong glue and partly stuck it on again. But it's not very firm now." [Passing, Piaget shrewdly points out that ambivalence toward fathers is on the whole less disturbing than ambivalence toward mothers; the father is often a nuisance but his removal is not so upsetting.]

Piaget's sensitivity to affective material is striking. For example, the case of the little girl who wants to cut off her father's head and then stick it on again, but not too firmly, denotes, he says, "how skillfully a balance can be achieved in symbolism between aggressiveness and its opposite, and how frequently in play the attitude to the father varies according to whether the parents are together or the father is alone (Piaget 1951). All those with whom the child lives generate affective schemas within the child's mind which represent a summary or blending of the various feelings aroused by them over developmental time. It is these schemas which determine the main secondary or unconscious symbols and help to explain later unreasonable attractions or antipathies.

The Gradual Intellectualization of Affect in Later Piaget

Piaget's approach to affective problems underwent a curious metamorphosis with age. Three fairly demarcated periods or phases can be distinguished:

1. In his earliest phase, he was still flirting with psychoanalysis, underwent a short trial analysis, and presented a paper at the 1922 International Congress of Psychoanalysis, with Freud as an attentive listener. Piaget himself was only 26 years old. The new terms that he was introducing, such as egocentrism, were related to existing psychoanalytic concepts such as narcissism and defined within the framework of psychoanalysis as "narcissism without Narcissus." He acknowledged his debt to Freud very generously. The Oedipus complex was described in strictly Freudian terms.

2. During his middle phase, Piaget came to the conclusion that psychoanalytic theory would profit immeasurably from being reformulated in Piagetian terms of schema, assimilation, and accomodation. The Oedipus complex, together with its "fixations," was now understood in a different way. Because of the first personal schemas, an individual may assimilate all subsequent people either to his father's schema or to his mother's schema. Because of the latter, he will tend to love in a certain way, sometimes all through his life, because he partially assimilates successive loves to his first love which shapes his innermost feelings and behavior (Piaget 1951). [You will notice that he is still making use of such intimate expressions as "love."] To quote him:

   A normal individual may find in his emotional life all kinds of traces of infantile behaviors connected with his relation to his mother. He will, however, add to them, and anyone who marries with a "mother fixation" runs the risk of considerable complications in his married life. Similarly, the man who continues throughout his life to be dominated by an idealized image of his father, . . . must of necessity have diminished powers. [Now comes the translation.] Equilibrium consists in preserving the living aspects of the past by continual accomodation to the manifold and irreducable present. (Piaget 1951)

3. In his third phase, Piaget moved futher away from psychoanalysis and further away from affect in the sense of normal human feelings. He now attempted a new translation of the Oedipus complex in more mathematical terms. The Oedipus stage, he said, represented a certain form of affective equilibrium, characterized by a maximization of "gains" expected from the mother and by a minimization of the "losses" expected from the father. It was a moot question as to whether the equilibrium point corresponded to a Bayes strategy, the criterion of which would be a simple maximum of "gains minus loss," or whether it corresponded to a "minimax" strategy with a search for the minimum or maximum loss which the subject supposed that a hostile environment was trying to inflict on him. The solution, of course, depended on the overall environmental conditions for each child. (Tanner and Inhelder 1960)

As his affect theory became less emotional, so the illustrations in his protocols grew more cognitive. In a comment I made a few years ago, I deplored the loss of those charming animistic children of long ago who talked about the world of dreams and shadows and thoughts so quaintly that psychologists all over the world became enthralled with this new conception of the child. Later, I said, this delightful creation was replaced by a Boolean monster who began talking the language of symbolic algebra without ever having obtained a single lesson in the subject.

Where Did the Affect Go?

The affect, as feeling, appeared to be disappearing gradually from Piaget's work as the years went by, although he still continued to acknowledge that it was always there by implication. He even began to postulate an intellectual unconscious to correspond with the Freudian unconscious with its own intellectual complexes, its own defenses against learning, and its own intellectual hang-ups. But if affect was the other side of the penny, the coin that Piaget began increasingly to use appeared to be double-headed so that it always landed with the cognitive side up.

One of the mysteries that intrigued me as a clinical interviewer was the absence of affect in the later protocols. How was it possible to keep it out unless one interrogated the child with almost scholastic rigor. I have come to the conclusion that it is well nigh impossible for a clinician to carry out Piaget's "clinical method" without simultaneously generating a good deal of affect during the process of problem solving. I will take as an example a protocol of a typical Piaget-type experiment conducted with a little girl who was asked to predict whether an array of objects would sink or float in the water.

> She misses two out of the first three predictions and begins to look embarrassed and then anxious and finally very ashamed of herself. When the next question is put to her, she recovers, comes smiling up to the examiner, and places an appealing and somewhat seductive hand on his shoulder. She shakes her head and says to him: "You don't want to be wrong again, do you? You want to be right this time, don't you? Why don't you just do it and see what happens?" On the cognitive side, she performed very much in keeping with Piaget's expectations but there were also some surprises that seemed related more to her affective than cognitive experience. On inquiry into her past history (tabooed in all Piaget studies) it appeared that she had suffered considerably at the hands of her teacher-mother who had constantly deflated her vulnerable little ego and was frequently punitive. By contrast, the father over-praised and over-stimulated the little girl so that she was often at a loss to know where the truth lay. (Anthony, in press)

There was no doubt that the truth in the experiment lay somewhere in the complex cognitive-affective process, in the past history of the little girl, in her present personality, and in the habitual ways that she had developed to defend herself against anxieties provoked by her two unbalanced parents and by her attempts to cope with the threats that every intellectual problem had come to represent for her. Piaget has never been interested in individual differences, let alone individual emotional differences. For him, every Genevese child was an average sort of child from an average expectable environment, giving an average sort of intellectual responses curiously devoid of any emotional involvement. Affect is there in all human activities if you look for it; if you don't look for it, it may not seem to be there.

Conclusion

It is by no means accidental that Piaget invented a "clinical method" for use in his investigations. His whole approach, especially in his earlier work, displays a sensitivity toward affect that is the hallmark of the true clinician. Clinicians can only resonate sympathetically to the stark honesty and directness of an individual who could refer to his "peculiar bent of character" that made him fundamentally a "worrier who only work can relieve" and who could speak of his "dissociation" as the means by which he has been able to "surmount a permanent fund of anxiety and transform it into a need for working." All these sensitive, autobiographical comments would indicate that he has as much insight into the workings of his own mind as he has of the minds of his subjects, and the insight is clearly not limited to the purely cognitive areas. As a final comment, I would like to quote from the end of a paper that appeared in the *Festschrift* celebrating Piaget's 70th birthday.

> It would seem that the clinical world lost a great clinician when Piaget, for personal reasons, turned his back on psychopathology, "depth" psychology, and the "tricks of the unconscious". The author, as a clinician, is not sure whether to be more sorry for what Piaget did not become or more happy for what he did become. On balance, he would not have had it any different and remains deeply grateful to the turn of the wheel that brought a Freud and a Piaget together in the same century to which he himself fortunately but undeservedly belongs. (Bresson and Montmollin 1966)

References

Anthony, E. J. "The System Makers: Piaget and Freud." *British Journal of Medical Psychology* 30 (1957): 255-269.

Anthony, E. J. "The Growth of Knowledge from the Developmental and Dynamic Points of View." In *Annals of Psychoanalysis,* edited by M. Basch. Chicago: Quadrangle, in press.

Bresson, F., and Montmollin, M. de. *Psychologie et Epistemologie Genetiques.* Paris: Dunod, 1966.

Dulit, E. "Adolescent Thinking a le Piaget: The Formal Stage." *Journal of Youth and Adolescence* 1 (1972): 281-301.

Evans, R. I. *Jean Piaget: The Man and His Ideas.* New York: Dutton, 1973.

Janet, P. *Psychological Healing: A Historical and Clinical Study.* Translated by Eden and Cedar Paul. New York: Macmillan, 1925.

Piaget, J. *The Moral Development of the Child.* London: Kegan, Paul, 1932.

Piaget, J. *Play, Dreams and Imitation in Childhood.* New York: Norton, 1951.

Piaget, J. *A History of Psychology in Autobiography,* edited by E. Boring. New York: Russell & Russell, 1952.

Piaget, J. "Les Relations entre l'Affectivite et l'Intelligence dans le Developpement Mental de l'Enfant." *Bulletin de Psychologie* 7 (1953).

Piaget, J. "The Affective Unconscious and the Cognitive Unconscious." *Journal of the American Psychoanalytic Association* 21 (1973): 249-261.

Tanner, J. S., and Inhelder, B. *Discussions on Child Development, Volume 4.* New York: International Universities Press, 1960.

When Children Talk Back— LISTEN!

A. Eugene Howard, *Professor, Early Childhood Education, Stephen F. Austin State University, Nacogdoches, Texas.*

How you and I perceive one another primarily determines how we interpret and respond to each other's behavior. Our perception of children determines how we interpret their behavior and respond to it. For example, two-year-old Jimmy hits his playmate over the head with a sand bucket. One of us may perceive this act as a result of the child's lack of cause-and-effect understanding, his egocentric inability to imagine the feelings of others, and his inadequately learned repertoire of appropriate responses in such social situations. The other may perceive the sand bucket assault as the result of natural antisocial or savage tendencies or as evidence of the child's innately sinful status which must be reformed. Our different perceptions of Jimmy and his behavior will lead each of us to respond quite differently to the child.

Adults in every society reflect in their behavior certain commonly held perceptions of themselves and their children. Each society holds rather tenaciously to certain feelings, values, and beliefs

—about the "nature" of children

"They're full of mischief."

"They are God's littlest angels."

"They're holy terrors."

—about what causes children to behave as they do

"What do you expect, she's an only child."
(or *the oldest* or *youngest* or *the child of working parents* or *deprived,* etc., etc., etc.)

"It's the Lord's will."

"The devil made him do it."

—and about what actions should be taken when persons behave in socially disapproved ways

"Let's just ignore her. We should pity people like that."

"He ought to be taken out and horsewhipped."

"What she needs is a good 'shrink.' "

Rarely is the efficacy of these feelings, values, and beliefs reliably or validly supported by objective research and scientific data. Generally, these perceptions are rooted deeply in unexamined folkways or in social and religious traditions of the society. Nevertheless, these perceptions are tacitly accepted as "the truth" about children and the treatment appropriate for them.

Whenever artists and scientists engaged in the objective study of child behavior and development propose new or different perspectives on the nature and treatment of children, many adults in the society react with intense skepticism or outright rejection. Thus, the growing body of reliable knowledge about optimal conditions for facilitating child growth, development, and learning has had a very limited impact on the childrearing, early education "industry." On the other hand, the discovery of a new plastic or a new process can quickly convert the procedures of a commercial industry. For example, recall how quickly the textile industry converted to the production of double knit or permanently-pressed fabrics.

In the arena of human "technology," we are not prone to act on the basis of what we know. Our behavior toward one another is fundamentally determined by what we feel, value, and believe. Of course, we sometimes allow what we know to affect our feelings, values, and beliefs—but only sometimes. A good illustration of this occurred recently when a kindergarten teacher came to me requesting help in dealing with a child who demonstrated frequent aggressive and attacking behavior. The teacher claimed to be at her wit's end. She professed to having used nearly every nonaggressive technique for changing the child's behavior. In her verbal and nonverbal behavior, however, she communicated covert hostility toward the child, although she refused to acknowledge this feeling openly. Later, I discovered that the teacher's primary techniques in responding to the child had consisted of bottom-swatting with her open palm, grasping the child by an arm or shoulder and mildly shaking him, and verbally moralizing about the rights and feelings of others. Although the teacher had acknowledged none of these behaviors in our conversations, her colleagues had frequently observed them.

I worked with the teacher for several weeks seeking ways to gain insight into the causes of the child's aggressive behavior. We learned that the child was consistently subject to attack by persons in his home. Spankings and cuffings were administered by his parents, brothers, sisters, and a grandparent for unexplained infractions of highly inconsistent "rules." The teacher and I looked into the research concerning the relationship between physical punishment by adults and agressive behavior in children. We recognized that the teacher's behavior was supporting his home treatment rather than counteracting it. Therefore, we began using nonaggressive methods which led to the reduction of aggressive behavior in the child.

Although the teacher evidenced knowledge of the research as well as practical methods of reducing the child's aggression, she failed to carry through in the use of that knowledge. Her perception and real needs were communicated to some colleagues in the teachers' lounge one day when the teacher said, "I don't care what the books say, it makes me furious to see him attack other children. He's simply going to learn that he can't get away with that in my classroom." The teacher continued to use her previous practices and the child persisted in his aggressive behavior, although he became more skilled in attacking when the teacher wasn't looking.

This teacher is no rarity. When it comes to interpreting and responding to children's behavior, our society is filled with people who righteously reject any scientific data and depend exclusively on those feelings, values, and beliefs based in tradition and custom. It is not uncommon to observe parents and teachers reacting with hostility toward any evidence that dares to refute their feelings, values, and beliefs.

The American Perception

In the American society, there is a common core of feelings, values, and beliefs held by an enormous number of adults. This core of perceptions transcends racial, ethnic, religious, and class differences and may be observed among individuals in nearly every group in the society. Fundamentally, this core of perceptions may be characterized as a negative or "Not OK" perception of children or of human beings in general. This core includes beliefs regarding the innately sinful, evil, or lost human condition; the basically antisocial "nature" of human beings, especially young ones; the acceptance of competition as the fundamental law of survival; and people as mechanical beings whose responses are shaped by stimulus prescriptions over which they have no willful control. These negatively-oriented beliefs, as well as others within the whole core of negative social perceptions of children, are unlikely to change until adults can debunk the half-truths and misinterpretations which have etched themselves so effectively into our customs and social beliefs.

In this society, I suggest that four major influences have converged in public thinking to forge an alliance of half-truths and misinterpretations which have become formidable roadblocks to changing our perceptions of ourselves and our children, of the causes of behavior, and of the means for interacting which will most probably allow us to develop into fully-functioning human beings. These four influences are:

1. **Christianity**—through its negative doctrine of human depravity and adherence to the "salvation" dogma;

2. **Freudian Theory**—through its emphasis on the basically antisocial nature of people and the hedonistic orientation of the child;

3. **Capitalism**—through its affiliation with Darwinian theory leading Americans to accept the "survival of the fittest" as the natural law to be applied to our social and economic relations;

4. **American Behaviorism**—through its simplistic view of the individual as a complex computer capable of being programmed without regard to human will and choice.

It is dangerous in a short presentation such as this to deal with such complicated and monumentally important forces without inviting misunderstanding. My words are subject to the reader's perceptions—to the feelings, values, and beliefs you bring to these pages—and therefore, subject to distortion of my intended message. Nevertheless, I shall brave the danger and forge ahead.

Negative Christian Doctrine

The impact of the Christian ethic on the world has included many positive and beneficial outcomes for individuals as well as for whole societies. Nonetheless, one influential tenet of Christianity has been and still remains its negative view of humanity. "In Adam's fall, we sinned all" was a maxim memorized by most young children in early America. The form of the message may have changed but the message itself remains unchanged. The writings of St. Augustine, John Calvin, Cotton Mather, and Billy Graham are packed with contentions that people are innately evil, lost, soiled, damned, and helpless to redeem themselves. Each Sunday morning in America, millions of children are progressively convinced of their "Not OK" status, especially in the "eyes of the Lord." Christian pulpits overflow with sermons depicting life as a battleground where opposing spirits vie for human souls—souls born, due to Adam's fall, into the hand of the evil one. Recent movies such as *The Exorcist* help popularize the notion that people are victims of possession without power to redeem themselves.

Further, our Puritan heritage still compels many Americans to an allegiance to punitive treatment as recompense for "evil" behavior. Sin must be punished. One can only attain goodness through suffering and the expiation of wrongdoing. "Spare the rod and spoil the child" is a phrase widely used as Biblical justification for adults to attack the bodies of children who behave in unaccepted ways. It is interesting to note, however, that this phrase does not appear in the Bible at all. However, in the passage from which this misquotation is bootlegged, Proverbs 13:24,* the Hebrew word for *rod* is the same word used in the familiar passage from the twenty-third Psalm (23:14) "Thy rod and Thy staff, they comfort me." *Rod* in these passages referred to a long slender reed used by a shepherd to direct his sheep away from danger. Only the most despised of shepherds beat his sheep; the rod was used to guide them toward safe passage into the field or the fold. The "sin" of a sheep was never expiated by violent application of the rod. Nevertheless, many pious Christians ignore this knowledge and cling to the misquoted misinterpretation which will support their need to justify their violence toward children.

---

*Authorized (King James) Version, Prov. 13:24. "He that spareth his rod hateth his son: but he that loveth him, chasteneth him betimes."

What You See Ain't Necessarily What You Got

Much of the so-called misbehavior of children appears in the light of objective analysis to be a response to their inappropriate treatment by adults. In my quarter century of child study, I have had the opportunity to observe a large sampling of child behavior. In a vast number of situations in which adults claim that children are misbehaving, I have been able to identify aspects of adult behavior which apparently triggered the unacceptable reactions of the child. To view this phenomenon another way, I have found that children's behavior is a kind of "TALK-BACK"—a feedback behavior by which the child, quite unintentionally, was cuing the adult to the inappropriateness of the adult's treatment. In recent years, studies of body language, transactional analysis, and behavior therapy have elevated our awareness of the extensive variety of nonverbal behaviors by which human beings seek to communicate ideas and feelings. "TALK-BACK" is my term for all those ways, verbal and nonverbal, by which young children seek to communicate the appropriateness or inappropriateness of adult behavior toward them.

The "TALK-BACK" of children can give us new insight into how we may improve the lot of children in this society. Unfortunately, many adults perceive this "TALK-BACK" as *prima facie* evidence of the child's innate evil and need for punitive controls. I am reminded of the mother who continued to spank her four-month-old son because he refused to stop crying when she ordered him to do so. She explained his behavior as being the result of his stubborn will which had to be broken lest the child would get the upper hand. I am also reminded of the nursery school teacher who refused to allow a four-year-old girl any special privileges as "helper" until the child quit showing off and trying to get attention. In this case, what the child desperately needed was willfully withheld until the child was willing to quit demonstrating her need in ways disapproved by the teacher. Again and again in homes and schools we can witness the "TALK-BACK" behavior interpreted as proof of depravity rather than as a cue for cure.

Our negative social view of childhood is a tragedy of major proportions. In this century we have attained knowledge about human behavior which, imperfect as it may be, is infinitely more helpful than unexamined traditions have been. Our growing understanding of the cause and effect relationships in child behavior and development provide us a reasonably reliable base upon which we can intelligently reexamine and revise our interpretations and perceptions. Our knowledge has the potential for transforming the negative orientations of the past and present into a more positive and constructive perspective in the future. This kind of transformation will remain unlikely, if not impossible, unless we are willing to allow what we know or can know to affect the deeply-rooted negative perceptions based in half-truth and misunderstanding.

Within the concerns of Christian theologians and laymen there is a fluctuating interest in a more positive view of people, in a reexamination of the meaning of salvation and sin. Certainly, within the broad concerns of social and biological research there is an emerging body of data which suggests that each person is basically a dynamic, integrated, constructively-oriented organism whose human prospects are positively directed. The questions before us are: What will it take to break the stranglehold of our negative religious perspectives and inject our feelings, values, and beliefs with a massive dose of positive perceptions? Can we move from the "Not OK" perception of children to the "I'm OK—Children are OK" perception which will reverse our whole system of social custom and tradition? Is it possible to emancipate ourselves from the tyranny of the doctrine of human depravity? I think so.

Freud's Theory

A second factor in the negative American perception of children lies in the influence of Sigmund Freud's theory on public beliefs. Although the heyday of Freud's popularity has passed, little argument exists regarding his residual impact on public thinking. Freud's work led many people to believe that the individual was naturally a selfish, id-oriented, hedonistic creature who evidenced self-destructive, antisocial tendencies. Such Freudian concepts found all too ready acceptance among Western thought which had already been oriented to negative aspects of Christian doctrine.

In the light of Freud's popular image, children were easily perceived as young savages, who, for the sake of society's survival, had to be civilized. Adults accepted the notion that they could never relent in their imposition of social control lest the savage nature of the child break through the thin veneer of human civilization. William Golding's novel *Lord of the Flies* promoted this frightening perception of child nature. In the grip of Freudian influence the child, already born in sin, was also perceived as antisocial, selfish, and hedonistic.

Despite the popular acceptance of this savage view of child nature, there is a considerable body of biological and psychological data which could convince us, if we dared to be convinced, that a person is at least no more antisocial than prosocial; that from conception the organism exhibits a developmental pattern positively oriented toward more cooperative social behavior, greater integrity, psychological continuity, and harmony, with a fundamental drive toward actualization of maximum possibilities.

Yet, do we dare question that which creates and sustains our negative perceptions, making us so resistant to positive knowledge about ourselves and our young? Is is possible to change ourselves and to convince others that a positive view of children has the potential for opening up a better future for us all? I think so.

Capitalism and Competition

During the time that the capitalistic system was shaping the United States into a major industrial and economic world power, an English naturalist, Charles Darwin, rocked the American public with his theory about the evolution of living species. Although in America the central storm of protest to Darwin's ideas focused around the Scopes's "Monkey" trial, a less notorious yet equally influential tenet of the theory was quietly being accepted. This tenet has been abbreviated and popularized in the phrase "survival of the fittest." This notion emerged from Darwin's observation that the weakest and least adaptable offspring in a species tended to die or be killed off in the balance of nature. In the hands of the American public, the idea was deformed into a belief in a natural force or bestial will which compelled animals to seek and destroy the weak. A "kill or be killed" image of nature emerged. The aggression which can be observed in nature became the focus of public belief. This myopia ignored the amount of nonruthless competition as well as the strong drives toward social and cooperative behavior which are also exhibited in the world of nature.

Disregarding the more balanced picture, Americans embraced the "savage-struggle-for-survival" image of nature. Not only did the public embrace the "red-in-tooth-and-fang" image of animals, they began to impose the idea upon their perceptions of themselves and of their social, political, and economic relations. Since only the fittest animals survived, the public assumed that only the fittest people, the fittest nations, the fittest workers, the fittest students *should be allowed* to survive or succeed. What had begun as one notion from a scientist's observations of natural functioning gradually was turned into a basis for social and educational practice in this country.

The focus on competiton for survival and success eclipsed the necessity of cooperation. Ruthless business, industrial, and educational practices were justified as expressions of human nature. First place was the only position worth holding in the competition. The biggest income, the finest home, the fanciest car, the most elaborate collection of goods became prime goals of the people in the world's newest industrial national giant. In time, however, this ruthless competition and its subsequent exploitation of people at home and of nations abroad contributed to the onset of a series of world crises and conflicts. The biologically "fittest" of our young men were sent off to die in war after war. This lopsided perspective of human nature had led to a complete reversal of the natural order which Darwin had observed.

Our overemphasis on competition led to the creation of an educational system which established age-level or grade-level academic and intellectual norms which children were obligated to attain. The schools established a system of internal competition through sorting and classifying children as "clods," "glitters," or as "faceless mediocrity." The system founded itself upon the assumption that all children should learn about the same things in about the same way at about the same time and pace. Those who could not succeed were originally failed, but lately they have been increasingly sorted out for placement in special classes where they are encouraged to compete with others identified as losers or defectives.

Grading, promotion and failure, grouping, and remediation are all vestiges of our deep-seated belief that competitive schooling will help our society sort out its fittest survivors. This misuse of competition has debilitating effects on children. These effects may be seen in the causes of many adolescent suicides, in the rise of mental illness among our children, in the psychological bruises often left on the losers in the Little League, the "Our Little Miss Pageant," or the imposed spelling bee.

Olympic Gold Medal winner Mark Spitz expressed the attitude generated by this malformed respect for competition. Several years ago in *Life Magazine,* Spitz was quoted as saying, "There's only one winner in the race. Everyone else in that pool is a bum." Only after his bitter defeat and humiliation in Mexico City was young Mr. Spitz able to reconstruct a cooperative, positive attitude which permitted him to perform so spectacularly in the Munich Olympics.

It seems clear to me that so much of the "TALK-BACK" behavior of children clearly indicates the inappropriate ways in which we adults have competitively constructed and constricted their lives. Yet, is there a way to put the virtues of competition and capitalism into more constructive perspective? Is there a way in which the "TALK-BACK" behavior of children can direct us out of the morass of bygone beliefs which hold us in place? I think so.

American Behaviorism

The last factor to be considered here as supporting and sustaining the negative American perception of children is the powerful influence which American behavioristic psychology has had on public thinking. I do not suggest that all contributions of behaviorism or Christianity, capitalism or Freudian theory have been negative. Indeed, behaviorism has contributed mightily to a better understanding of people. The negative influence of this nontheory theory occurred rather subtly to begin with. Behaviorists constructed a simple and mechanistic model of behavior for the sake of achieving the scientific precision which would emancipate psychology from its messy predecessor, philosophy. What began as a limited perspective considered necessary for rigorously controlled scientific research all too rapidly was embraced as a true and accurate model of the dynamics of human behavior and learning. The twentieth century human being was introduced as a kind of psychological blank slate upon which a series of stimulus and response connections mechanically constructed patterns of behavior. Any nonobservable or internal mediating forces were rejected as being scientifically unverifiable. The simplistic stimulus and response paradigm allegedly could be objectively controlled in experiments with either adults or children. It was assumed that the "meaning" of the stimulus would be the same for the child as for the adult. In making this assumption, behaviorists resurrected a modern version of the "miniature adult" theory. Children were only small adults in regard to the validity of the stimulus-response paradigm. The functioning intellect of the child was believed to be like that of the adult only less filled with "content" (S-R connections), less experienced, or less able to coordinate the S-R connections which had been etched upon the blank slate of the infant's "mind."

Behaviorists popularized formal schooling as a process of breaking down all learning into micro-stimulus-response associations, sequencing the presentation of these microlessons and rewarding correct responses of the child. This notion was a model for teaching, not for learning. The idea based itself in the assumption that teaching procedures which presented stimuli in an order compatible with adult logic would certainly be the most effective and productive means of eliciting psychological or intellectual development in the child. In practice, the assumption has proved shaky at best and damaging to children at worst.

Considerable evidence exists to convince us, if we dare to be convinced, that the teaching procedures which are so beautifully structured by adult logic are not equally as attractive in their effects on children's learning. Evidence suggests that the young child's structures of thinking, for constructing meaning from reality, are distinctly different from those of adults. These differences appear to stem from both a qualitative and quantitative difference in the functioning of adult and child intellect. The young child's thinking is not only different in content (what has been experienced) but also in function (in the ways the brain can give meaning to experience). Piaget has opened up new perspectives on thinking and learning which give challenge to the dominating forces of American behaviorism.

The negative results of behaviorism are also seen when behaviorists' research has been prematurely and inappropriately moved from the laboratory to the classroom. Procedures which worked with cats, rats, and pigeons have not always been so successful in a class of five-year-old children. Some behavioristic school programs may have actually impeded the later developmental progress of the children involved. Worst of all, when the highly touted power of programmed learning fizzled, children and teachers were blamed for its failure. As one teacher said at the beginning of the year, "If these kids can't learn with these beautifully organized lessons, they are really hopeless." At the end of the year, when it was discovered that no significant progress had been made by the "programmed" children as compared to a matched group using other procedures and materials, the teacher was heard to complain, "I don't know why they hold me accountable for this mess. I did everything I was told to do. Why do I get blamed when the idiots in the front office pick the wrong materials?"

One may think it unfair of me to charge behaviorism with the negative outcomes of its misuse. Nevertheless, the behaviorist's mechanistic view of learning and the premature application of laboratory procedures to classroom instruction has led to blaming children for failing to fulfill behaviorists' expectations. Behavioral objectives and the mechanistic model for teaching which was advanced have failed to meet the needs of far too many children. Tragically, when the failure occurs, it is the children and not the defective model who are blamed for the failing.

The "TALK-BACK" response of children in many of these mechanistic educational situations has been filled with messages of boredom, frustration, anxiety, and despondency. Unfortunately, parents and teachers have often interpreted this "TALK-BACK" as verification of the child's intellectual inability and recalcitrant resistance to being civilized, rather than as cues to the inappropriateness of the entire approach to thinking and learning in school. Nevertheless, can this behaviorist overdomination be alleviated? I think so.

Listening to "TALK-BACK"

The "TALK-BACK" behavior of children can clue us to the inappropriateness of our behavior toward them if we know how to read it objectively. Likewise, our own "TALK-BACK" behavior toward children, if we dare to read it honestly, may cue us to better understanding of ourselves. The best way to improve our perception of children and to help them is to improve our self perception and to help ourselves. We cannot find ways to change our negative perceptions of children until we admit that we are responsible for choosing those perceptions—until we admit that we have listened for what we wanted to hear, have interpreted as we were wont to interpret.

In order to survive psychologically, each of us must be able to predict and to some extent control our immediate environment. Our negative perceptions of children serve our need to control and predict human behavior in keeping with our childhood learning about ourselves. We select these negative causes because they do not disturb our psychological set. It is easier to blame conditions over which we believe we have no control and against which we can do nothing than it is to accept responsibility for our choices and, thereby, acknowledge our power to change them.

In order to change, we must first be willing to analyze our feelings and choices and to give up the payoffs which our negative perceptions provide us. Change will cause us uncertainty and distress. We are not likely to subject ourselves to this kind of stress until we are grossly and genuinely dissatisfied with the outcomes of our negative perceptions on the lives of children and on our own personal fulfillment. We must dare to acknowledge the destructiveness of our negative perceptions before we will seek more positive ones. We can choose to reject the negative payoffs from Puritan ethics, Freudian tenets, social Darwinism, and the mechanistic view of humanity without will or volition. If we so dare, it is realistically possible to view ourselves and our children positively and to predict and control our environment in infinitely more satisfying ways.

Our negative perceptions of children flow from negative perceptions of ourselves, from deep-seated beliefs that people are more effectively improved through the trauma of hardship and pain than through the experience of love and joy. As a result, from infancy onward, many of us develop a need for punishment, a sense of our duty to suffer, to be meek and lowly, and an inalienable right to unjust treatment. When we attain parenthood or a position in which we have the responsibility for the care and rearing of children, we feel compelled to socialize the child in our own "ideal-image." The child thereby becomes the sacrificial dove, the Paschal Lamb, the whipping boy to bear the burden of our guilt. In punishing the child, we satisfy our unfulfilled needs for punishment. In negatively talking about children, we confess the absence of our own fulfillment. By chastising or otherwise downing a child, we express a perverted commitment to perfecting the next generation in the image of our faults. The fact that the practices we employ prohibit the maximal fulfillment of both child and adult seems not to affect us at all.

The child who attacks others exhibits "TALK-BACK" that cries out for loving "strokes," for the "warm fuzzies" of someone's true caring, for the establishment of consistent limits that give security and support, for help in discovering satisfying ways of expressing frustration and anger. If, instead of "warm fuzzies," the child is subjected to "cold pricklies"—to attack for attacking, to belittling moralization, to guilt-elevating lectures and sermons on the virtue of rules, commandments, regulations, or law and order—we may expect even more disturbing "TALK-BACK" from the child. To hear the real meaning of "TALK-BACK" we must be able to emotionally disengage ourselves from the medium of the message. This ability to read "TALK-BACK" accurately demands careful attention to the consequences of the "TALK-BACK" we are observing—not to what the child actually says or does but to the actual consequences of the behavior. The child who claims to want friends but continues to drive away every child who expresses friendship is communicating the message, "I'm not OK, nobody likes me, and you've got to dislike me too, otherwise I won't know how to feel about myself."

Our most deeply-rooted needs and those of children tend to be hidden. Children and adults often work diligently, though unconsciously, to achieve goals which they claim not to want. The kindergarten teacher referred to earlier in this paper claimed that she did not want Jimmy to be aggressive. Her behavior clearly told Jimmy to continue his aggression so that her need to punish and Jimmy's need to be punished could continue to be fulfilled without disruption. Disrupting the "game" would have been distressing to both teacher and child.

The secret to changing our behavior or that of children is to realize that any individual can change, but that one can change another only by motivating the other to change himself. As parents and teachers, we have the advantage of being able, if we choose, to understand the "TALK-BACK" behavior of children. The young child, however, is not yet able to deal objectively with such abstractions. Therefore, those who have the ability to change must accept the primary responsibility for the transformation which is so sorely needed.

The change is possible—

- if we dare to doubt the validity of our negative perceptions;
- if we refuse to listen only for what we want to hear;
- if we disengage our emotional reactions to what is said or done and focus our attention on the actual consequences of "TALK-BACK";
- if we are willing to pass through a period of uncertainty and psychological distress;
- if we refuse to respond to "TALK-BACK" in the expected way, but instead react with a creative response—one that does not follow precedents, that does not advance the "game" but which causes uncertainty in the child, who then can begin to search for new ways of responding.

Children are the last slaves in our society. They have borne for too long the heavy burdens of this society's Puritanical, antisocial, mechanistic, and savagely competitive view of itself. In a constructive interpretation of the "TALK-BACK" of our children lies the seeds of a renaissance in our understanding of people and in our fulfillment of our greatest human potential. We can choose to be free to reinterpret that "TALK-BACK" in positive ways. We can choose to decide that personal behavior and development is more satisfyingly guided by "warm fuzzies" than by "cold pricklies."

Preschool and Early Math Instruction: A Developmental Approach

Donald T. Streets, *Associate Director, Center for the Study of Human Potential, School of Education, University of Massachusetts, Amherst, Massachusetts.*

Imagine yourself observing a traditional classroom during math period. What do you suppose would be going on? You might hear the entire class chanting responses to the teacher's rapid-fire presentation of addition or subtraction facts. Or you might see all the children working on the same page of a workbook containing row after row of numerical combinations. The teacher very likely would have readily available ditto sheets of problems similar to those found in the workbook assignment for children unfortunate enough to have completed their assignment before the end of the period.

Now, imagine yourself in a classroom where modern math is being taught. What do you suppose would be a typical lesson? The following example might serve as a prototype.

[The teacher asks:] "Why is 2 + 3 = 3 + 2?"

Unhesitatingly the students reply, "Because both equal 5."

"No," reproves the teacher, "the correct answer is because the commutative law of addition holds."

Her next question is, "Why is 9 + 2 = 11?"

Again the students respond at once: "9 and 1 are 10 and 1 more is 11."

"Wrong," the teacher exclaims. "The correct answer is that by the definition of 2, 9 + (1 + 1) = (9 + 1) +1. Now, 9 + 1 is 10 by the definition of 10 and 10 + 1 is 11 by the definition of 11." (Kline 1973, p.1)

Shortcomings of Traditional and Modern Math Approaches

Of course, neither of these examples represents the best of either the traditional or modern math programs in some of our schools; our outstanding technological achievement is partial evidence that whatever methods have been used in math instruction have at least benefited some individuals.

What are the problems inherent in the traditional approach to teaching mathematics? Probably the most fundamental weakness is the tendency of teachers to force the student to solve problems by relying on the rote memorization of algorithms to given problems rather than on the attainment of a fundamental understanding of the problem and how to solve it (Kline 1973, p. 4). Most first grade texts require the child not only to use mathematical symbolic representations apart from their concrete referents, but also to arrange those abstractions in elaborate algebraic formulas, and then render the answers. Analyses by developmental psychologists of the cognitive competence necessary to understand such sets of abstractions indicate that this kind of assignment is beyond the grasp of most first graders (Lovell 1971, p. 14). And yet, in the face of their students' repeated failures, teachers continue to expect this of them. Why? Because most teachers see no alternative to using the textbook as a guide; they continue to teach all children the same lesson at the same time irrespective of individual differences.

Another flaw in traditional math instruction is the teacher's failure to relate math content to the experiences and interests of the child, both past and present. Experiences assimilable by young children are largely concrete; consequently, when information of a semiabstract or abstract nature is presented to them, they usually do not see how it relates to that base of experience (Ausubel 1970, p. 47). Therefore, abstractions have little or no meaning to children. The meaning that a child draws from experience is also influenced by the extent to which continuity is represented in his or her math experiences. For learning free of failure to take place, prerequisites for a given learning experience must be mastered first. When math materials and lessons are not sequenced properly (simple to complex; concrete to abstract) or are unrelated to the child's interests, then failure is virtually guaranteed (Kline 1973, p. 6).

Because traditional math materials deal primarily with numbers and doing exercises, they do not "connect" with the child's background or present interests. Just one brief glance at typical traditional math materials, particularly the books, reveals that they are insufferably dull (Kline 1973, p. 13). They contain page after page of arithmetic examples with a few problems interspersed, most of which are foreign to the child's real life situation.

The most fundamental inadequacy of traditional math, however, is that it does not even take into account, let alone facilitate, the emergence of the cognitive structures a child must develop in order to grasp the meaning that underlies number relations.

A little over ten years ago, parents and educators alike were led to believe that, with the advent of modern math, a virtual renaissance in math instruction was in the making. Workshops were springing up everywhere, with universities vying with each other to be the first to offer a full-blown course in modern math and its instruction. While the movement did serve to highlight the deplorable condition of math instruction in this country, modern math hardly represents a substantial improvement over the traditional approach.

What are some of the fundamental shortcomings of modern math? First of all, as with traditional math, modern math programs require logic and reasoning far beyond the child's cognitive capabilities. There is a heavy reliance on the use of definitions and axioms to make mathematical deductions (Kline 1973, pp. 24-50).

Set theory requires a sophisticated level of classificatory behavior, including such concepts as the union of sets (5 books + 4 lemons = 9 objects); the intersection of sets (5 books, one of which is red, and 3 red objects, one of which is a book—the red books being the intersection of those two sets); subsets (red chairs as a subset of chairs); empty sets (past U.S. presidents who were women); and infinite and natural numbers. The premature introduction of set theory represents yet another dimension of the disparity between the expectations of modern math instructors and the cognitive capability of the students (Kline 1973, p. 92).

A second and fatal mistake is the use of language too abstract for the child and too far removed from the child's vocabulary (Kline 1973, pp. 60-73). Appropriate use of such terms as commutative, associative, and distributive to describe properties of various mathematical operations is expected of youngsters too immature linguistically to understand their meaning.

Related to the problem of language is the assumption of modern math educators that the concrete referents of the mathematical abstractions being presented would be automatically seen and understood by the child (Kline 1973, p. 20). This, however, is not the case, and successful early education professionals are realizing that children need to have experience with concrete objects before they can manipulate symbols, and that they need to return to the concrete experience to ensure that they, indeed, make the connection.

The framers of the modern math approach have exacerbated their inadequacies by ignoring the role of pedagogy in the educative process. (Kline 1973, p. 131). An example of this is represented in their assumption that a mere parsimonious, succinct, symbolic presentation of information is all that is necessary to get children to understand math (Kline 1973, p. 132). This error is in part due to the lack of experience the framers of modern math as pure mathematicians have had with children and with math teachers. Implicit in their scheme is the assumption that children learn math just as adults do. In other words, they assume that the best approach to math instruction is precisely the approach they use as math theoreticians, even though they themselves did not learn math in that way.

Morris Kline (1973) questions the competence of math theoreticians to serve in a leadership role in revamping math instruction because they have misguided the field of math itself for quite some time. He claims that they have abandoned science, the discipline which gave rise to the need for the development of mathematics, and are now pursuing more selective and obscure abstractions unrelated to concrete reality (Kline 1973, p. 126). Modern math theorists tend to know very little about the fields of physics and engineering, while in the past the purpose of math was to serve these areas. This concern for the isolation of math instruction from experience has led Alfred N. Whitehead to state: "There can be nothing more destructive of true education than to spend long hours in the acquirement of ideas and methods which lead nowhere . . . "(Whitehead 1964, p. 189).

In summary, many of the shortcomings of the traditional approach are also found in the modern math program. Both fail to recognize that, at a very early age, children learn quantitative relationships basically through an inductive approach. It is simply beyond children at that developmental level to understand theoretical propositions, definitions, or axioms, use them as premises, and make logical deductions from them. Rather, their approach to understanding is to extract (induce) concepts from concrete experience and then ultimately apply them to similar situations. Only at a later developmental stage when they are capable of formal logic can they use a deductive inferential mode of thought.

Secondly, the language that is used must be comprehensible to the child. A major fault of instruction is the unwarranted assumption by teachers that children understand the meanings of the words they use. The greatest weakness, however, in both the traditional and the modern math programs is the failure to match the math learning experience with each child's developmental level. To do this requires the application of a theory of development and theories of teaching and curriculum consistent with it. This is precisely the challenge the Anisa Model addresses.

The Anisa Model

For the past fourteen years, the Anisa staff has been wrestling with the task of conceptualizing a developmentally-based educational system that not only provides the remedy for the ills just mentioned in math instruction, but those related to the total education of the child as well. Traditional education is characterized by activities in which children are required to memorize facts, mostly for the purpose of retrieving them for an exam. The rapid increase in knowledge and technology has made this approach obsolete. Microphotography, for instance, has been developed to the point where the entire Encyclopaedia Brittanica can be represented on a piece of microfilm the size of a 3 x 5 card. Factual information is doubling every eight years. Our educational systems are literally collapsing because of their inability to handle the information explosion and the rapid social change which accompanies it. This is one of many reasons why Anisa initiated a massive research effort fourteen years ago to create an alternative system of education that does far more than merely disseminate facts. This effort included an intensive investigation into both Eastern and Western philosophical thought, from philosophers predating Plato to those of the twentieth century.

Why was such an investigation necessary? The educational profession has recently experienced a proliferation of "innovative" schemes and ideas, mostly piecemeal efforts designed in ignorance of the nature of those for whom the innovations were intended. To avoid these pitfalls, a comprehensive approach to education was needed, one that would necessarily involve gathering together and organizing into a coherent scheme all of the pertinent data about human growth and development. However, at present, that body of information is fragmented, incomplete, and, in many instances, contradictory and somewhat confusing. Other attempts to integrate it have failed. We believe that this failure is largely due to the absence of a wider conceptual framework. Since the purpose of philosophy is to disclose the nature of something, a philosophical base of the Model was developed to provide a view of the nature of human beings and serve as a broad conceptual framework in which all the information about human growth and development might be organized and systematized into one, coherent, comprehensive scheme.

While it is beyond the purpose of this paper to fully explicate in detail the philosophical and theoretical underpinnings of the Anisa Model, it is important to present at least the broad strokes of that conceptual framework from which the Anisa approach to math instruction has been derived.

The philosophical foundation of the Model has been heavily influenced by the writings of Alfred North Whitehead, whose cosmology represents a unique synthesis of both Eastern and Western thought. This philosophical base identifies the fundamental propositions or assumptions about the nature of humanity which serve as the first principles of education. Because they are consistent with the fundamental principles of evolution, they enable us to determine our own future when properly understood and applied. Scientists have long known that the best way to make use of a fundamental law is to obey it (apply it). By applying the laws of aerodynamics, for example, we are not only able to travel from continent to continent, but interplanetary travel is also within our grasp. The same thing holds true for basic principles related to human nature.

Therefore, one of the fundamental principles of the Anisa Model identifies human potentialities as limitless. So long as the biological integrity of the human organism is functioning properly, there is no time during which the individual cannot learn something new. Each new bit of learning then increases one's capabilities for learning even more. Potential, therefore, can be created and in this sense is limitless. This is not to deny that one's genetic endowment is determined at conception. But the limit of that endowment's expression has never been conceptualized in science because of the human ability to create further potential.

A second fundamental proposition related to human nature is that reality inheres in the process of one's becoming. Whitehead indicates that the fundamental characteristic underlying the entire universe is change. Change can, however, be in two directions: toward increased entropy—which refers to change in the direction of randomness, a winding down; and toward increased order (negative entropy)—which is change away from randomness involving the reorganization of differentiated elements into higher levels of complexity, a process of evolution—a building up rather than a winding down. In humans, the process of creating more complex structures is essentially what is meant by the term "development." It is fundamental to survival because it enables the growing individual to deal more and more effectively with the environment over time, thereby becoming progressively more adaptive. Once you acknowledge that creation is characterized by change or process and not by static actuality, you presuppose potentiality; all of creation is changing from what it now is to what it potentially can be. The translation of potentiality into actuality, as defined by the philosophical basis of the Model, characterizes all growth and development in humans, and constitutes the essential dynamics of creativity.

A proposition of the Anisa theory of development identifies interaction with the environment as the means by which the process of translating potentiality into actuality is sustained. Therefore, the quality of the environment and the child's interaction with it are critical to the quality and speed of the child's growth and development. The philosophical affirmation that human potentialities are limitless poses a problem when it comes to identifying them for practical purposes. This difficulty was resolved by setting up categories by which all potentialities might be organized. The initial grouping identified two broad categories of potentiality—biological and psychological. The theory of development establishes *nutrition* as the key factor in the release of the biological potentialities and *learning* as the key factor in the release of the psychological potentialities. A child's learning is impaired if he is not healthy and if he suffers from malnutrition (Raman 1975).

Psychological potentialities have been categorized further into five areas: (1) psychomotor—which refers to the organization, movement, and control of the voluntary muscles; (2) perception—the organization of sensory stimuli, both internal and external, into recognizable patterns for interpretation; (3) cognition—which refers to thinking; (4) affective—the organization of feelings and emotions; and, (5) volition—the ability to formulate intentions and follow them through to satisfactory completion. Within each of these categories the main processes germane to the attainment of learning competence have been identified, defined, elaborately described, and theoretically justified. Developmental data pertinent to these processes have been compiled and a list of educational objectives derived from them has been articulated. Prototypical experiences which facilitate their development have been designed and tested.

A systematic investigation of all the extant theories of learning led to the identification of the basic elements characteristic of all known forms of learning, namely, *differentiation, integration,* and *generalization.* Learning, broadly defined, is the ability *to differentiate* elements of experience (psychomotor, perceptual, cognitive, affective, and volitional experiences) and *to integrate* those elements at a higher level of complexity and ultimately *to generalize* the integrations to other similar situations. Learning competence is the *conscious* ability to differentiate, integrate, and generalize. Becoming a competent learner is the ever-present objective of the child in an Anisa school. When children become competent learners, they are then in charge of their own destinies.

The processes which have been identified in each of the categories of potentiality are too numerous to mention here, but suffice it to say that they are ordered expressions of the energy of the individual in particular ways; they are not random expressions. For example, one process in the cognitive domain is classification, an ordered expression of the thinking potentialities of the organism to categorize or group items on the basis of a shared attribute or a set of shared attributes. Since attempting to deal with every stimulus on an ad hoc basis is beyond the capabilities of any human being, the ability to classify is imperative. It enables the individual to simplify his environment and therefore make sense out of it. We have thus far identified most of the pertinent processes in each of the five categories of potentiality and have developed a curriculum to strengthen each of them.

If development is defined broadly as the translation of potentiality into actuality, and interaction with the environment is the means by which that process is sustained, then teaching must be defined as *arranging environments* and *guiding the child's interaction* with those environments to achieve the objectives of the curriculum. Thus, an appraisal of any teaching act can be based on the extent to which the arrangement of the environment and the guidance of the child's interaction with it are appropriate to the objective in mind, and the degree to which the teacher facilitates the child's differentiating the elements comprising the experience, integrating those elements at a higher level, and then generalizing the integration to other situations.

The Anisa theory of curriculum is also a logical derivative of the theory of development and is defined as two sets of objectives, *content objectives* (which concern information about the world in which the child lives), and *process objectives* (which concern the development of learning competence in each of the categories of potentiality), *and what children do,* usually with the assistance of another person, *to achieve those objectives.* As content is assimilated and processes are mastered, the potentialities of the child are actualized.

There are three basic environments with which the child necessarily must interact: (1) the physical environment, which we define as everything represented in the ontological levels below humanity—animal, vegetable, and mineral; (2) the human environment—comprising all humans; and (3) the environment of unknowns—all of the unknowns one is aware of by virtue of consciousness, such as one's mortality; the future, what one is capable of becoming (unactualized potentialities); and most fundamentally, the ultimate mysteries in the universe.

When the human organism interacts with each of these environments, he responds as a total human being comprised of a biological self, capable of movement, perceptions, thoughts, feelings, and certain intentions. As he interacts, these learning capabilities function in a collaborative way, creating structures (patterned uses of energy) which comprise that particular environment. We have defined these structured patterns as *attitudes* and *values.* It is the role of education to guide the formation of attitudes and values in a way that brings the individual closer to the realities of those three environments and prevents his becoming out of touch with their essential nature.

The human capacity for abstraction has led to the utilization of basic symbol systems in structuring our relation to these three environments. For the material environment, math serves as a primary symbol system; for the human environment, language is the main symbol system for the interactional process; and for the environment of unknowns, art serves as the symbol system for attempting to present "visions" of possibilities—the unknown things we might become. The environments represent in themselves a hierarchy consistent with the various ontological levels specified by Whitehead (mineral, vegetable, animal, human, unknowns), and each higher level includes the properties of the lower (i.e., the human environment includes the properties of the material environment and the unknown includes those of both the human and material environments).

One particular property of any element of any of the three environments (whether mineral, vegetable, animal, etc.), is the capacity for internal factors of the element to determine to some extent its own behavior. In other words, one is unable to predict the behavior of elements of any of the environments entirely on the basis of external factors—a quality physicists came to understand about the material world when they rejected the mechanistic view of the universe in favor of an organismic view, a quality in human beings behaviorists in psychology still do not acknowledge. The principle which describes the internal determinants governing the activity of the components of each of the environments has been referred to as the subjectivist principle or principle of indeterminacy. It indicates that the amount of "indeterminacy" is increased with each higher ontological level. In other words, plants have more "self-determination" than rocks; animals have more than plants; and humans have more than rocks, plants, or animals. The symbol systems used by humans to mediate experience with the three environments—math, language, and the arts—accommodate the increased indeterminacy of each higher ontological level.

Each individual, then, has some say in how he will behave—how he will use his energies. As each individual interacts with the various environments over time, he uses the symbol systems to help establish relatively enduring patterns of energy use. In the Anisa Model, these patterns of energy use define the individual's values. To the degree that these values put him in touch with the essential realities of the physical, the human, and unknown environments, he will attain technological competence, moral competence, and aesthetic or spiritual competence, respectively. Spiritual competence is defined in psychological rather than religious or denominational terms and refers to the human capacity to approach unknowns or forming hypotheses or ideals which enable him to deal with his own mortality, his future, and the ultimate mysteries of the cosmos.

Developmental Prerequisites to Understanding Number

Math plays a critical role in the actualization of human potentialities because it enables one to come to grips with quantity—an ever-present part of the reality of any existing thing. Technological competence is impossible without the ability to understand the quantitative realities of the physical environment through the symbol system of math. Since math is essentially a cognitive activity, there are several basic cognitive processes which constitute the developmental prerequisites to understanding number relations—prerequisites to grasping the meaning of mathematical thought.

According to Piaget and many of his followers, there are four processes in the cognitive domain that have been determined to be particularly pertinent to understanding number relations. They are: *classification, seriation, transitivity,* and *conservation.*

Classification refers to the ability to group objects, actions, feelings, events, or ideas on the basis of their recognized similarities. To classify, one has to decide which items belong in a particular group or class by virtue of its possessing a property or properties which are the critieria which define the class. Classification makes sense out of experience because it reduces the complexities of the environment by ordering it into categories (Bruner, Goodnow, and Austin 1956). Can you imagine dealing with everything on an ad hoc basis? Suppose you had to confront every set of stimuli which we call "chair" on an individual basis, identifying and labeling each chair encountered individually rather than as a collection. It would be impossible to communicate to anyone else a particular "chair" experience. Only when one can abstract the properties which constitute "chairness" and represent them with a label symbolizing the same meaning can we effectively make sense out of "chair" experiences and communicate those experiences to others.

Developmentally, there are three basic types of classification: (1) *perceptual*—which is sorting items based on physical attributes such as color, shape, size, pitch, and texture (classification that is largely the result of perception tends to remain unchanged by subsequent experience); (2) *conceptual*—which refers to grouping items on the basis of function (this is largely determined by social knowledge from the culture such as things which are eaten, things you can ride on, or things that are worn); and, (3) *abstract conceptual*—which involves organizing events or ideas on the basis of a scheme which necessarily requires logical thought. It is this latter form of classification that tends to be modified, formed, and re-formed on the basis of logical processes.

There are different stages of classification. The first stage which might be considered a preclassificatory level is called *heaping.* This is when the child indiscriminately groups items on piles. The next stage is called *graphic collections*—organizing items on the basis of shifting criteria such as starting with the grouping of items using red as a criterion. The first item is red; the second is red and square. The criterion then shifts from red to squareness. The third item is a square that is yellow. The next item may be the same size as the yellow items. The graphic collections stage is followed by *simple sorting*—grouping objects according to a single property that is perceptually apparent such as color, shape, pitch, size, and texture. The fourth stage of classification is called *true classification;* in this stage the child is able to group objects by abstracting a property common to them all and to include all objects which fit into that category. The stage of *multiple classification* which follows involves classifying on the basis of more than one attribute or property and recognizing that an object can belong to several classes at the same time. For example, the criteria for classification may be the attributes of redness and squareness. The highest form of classification is called *class inclusion.* It involves forming subclasses of objects and including the subclasses in a larger class. For example, the contents of a bag of red and yellow wooden beads can be seen to have three classes: the two subclasses of red beads and yellow beads, and the inclusive class, wooden beads, to which they all belong.

Classification is not only important because it reduces the complexity of the world so that it can be dealt with in a manageable way, it is also important, according to Bruner, because almost all other cognitive activity presupposes the ability to group events according to their class.

Seriation refers to the ability to arrange items on the basis of their recognized differences. *Simple seriation* is ordering items on the basis of one dimension such as height, width, intensity of color, or pitch. *Multiple seriation* is simultaneously ordering items in a series on the basis of the predetermined dimensions, such as height, and width where the tallest and fattest would be the first in the series and the shortest and thinnest would be the last.

From a developmental point of view, seriation starts in a very global way by perceptually differentiating qualitative attributes of items such as color or size and identifying polarities such as big, small; loud, soft; long, short; fat, thin; etc. *Perceptual seriation* refers to the ability to order things on the basis of obvious, perceptually recognized differences. *Intuitive, progressive seriation and correspondence* (pairing items) refer to the ability to construct a series with a certain amount of trial and error effort without the intervention of another person. Concrete operational seriation refers to the ability to order objects without hesitation or the use of trial and error methods. *Ordinal correspondence* refers to the ability to integrate ordinal and cardinal relationships between the elements in two series of items. A child who has mastered this understands that in the series 1, 2, 3, 4, 5, the "3" represents both the third position (ordinality) and has the numerical value 3 (cardinality). Here we see the relationship between classification and seriation with respect to understanding number: the abstract quantitative attribute of a group is the class (its cardinal aspect), and the order of that class with respect to other items in the series, based on the recognized differences between them, is the result of seriation (the ordinal aspect of number).

Furthermore, seriation and classification tasks often entail understanding some kind of *correspondence* between two sets of items. Correspondence involves pairing objects on the basis of some common relationship among the pairs. The nature of this relationship is dependent upon whether correspondence is combined with a symmetrical or asymmetrical order. If the relationship is symmetrical (e.g., four identical apples paired with four identical dishes), the child performing the task could pair any apple with any dish, discovering in the process four pairs of elements. Because the pairs are equivalent (each apple-and-dish pair is like the others), the order involving classification is irrelevant. This is cardinal correspondence since the pairing is established irrespective of order.

When correspondence is combined with an asymmetrical order of graded differences (seriation), the nature of the pairing is determined by the position of each element in the series (e.g., five flowers of graded sizes paired with five vases of graded sizes). As Piaget (1965) states:

> . . . number is organized, stage after stage, in close connection with the gradual elaboration of systems of inclusions (hierarchy of logical classes) and systems of asymmetrical relations (qualitative seriations), the sequence of numbers thus resulting from an operational synthesis of classification and seriation. (p. viii)

Transitivity, implicit in seriation, is the process of inferring the quantitative relationship between two numbers from knowledge of the relationship they have with a third number. The simplest form is *transitivity of equivalence.* If John is as tall as Joan, and John is as tall as Jerry, then Joan and Jerry are the same height (A = B; A = C; therefore, B = C). A more complex form is *transitivity on the basis of differences.* If Mary is heavier than George, and George is heavier than Mark, then Mary must be heavier than Mark. Take the following illustration of serial ordering—

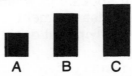

Since C is larger than B, one knows that C is larger than A through knowledge of B's relationship with A.

It is not known whether transitivity or seriation comes first in the development of the child, or which one strengthens the other. However, there does seem to be a sequence in the development of transitivity, with transitivity of equivalence preceding differences, and with the transitive inference based on the concept "greater than" coming before the transitive inference based on the concept "less than." According to Piaget, transitivity is a universal process which is implicated in practically all other forms of inference. Transitive relationships involving color and form are easier to discern than those involving height, weight, and number. Because children approximately nine years of age are capable of reversibility of thought, they should be able to handle transitive relationships on all levels using verbal cues rather than having items or numbers in question visually present.

Conservation is the process of reasoning that enables one to understand that certain attributes (qualitative and quantitative) remain the same or invariant while certain other attributes undergo transformation. In order for a person to understand conservation, one must recognize and establish equality between the data being considered (weight, volume, area, or number) before and after the transformation has taken place. Conservation presupposes being able to reverse a mental act in the following ways: (1) *inversion or negation,* which refers to cancelling an operation by combining the original operation with its opposite; (2) *reciprocity,* which refers to equalizing an operation by introducing an off-setting factor to compensate for the original change. There are several types of conservation: (a) mass or substance; (b) weight (same as above, but a scale is introduced); (c) length; (d) number; (e) continuous quantity; (f) discontinuous quantity; (g) order; and (h) area.

Why is conservation necessary? According to Piaget, conservation is basic to reasoning because reasoning requires permanence or consistency of definitions. Words presented here have to mean the same thing when presented again elsewhere. In the area of quantitative relationships, fiveness must equal fiveness, irrespective of where it is found and apart from its concrete referrents; otherwise the prospects of even beginning to understand the meaning of quantity is impossible. In other words, number is only intelligible if it remains identical to itself wherever it appears in whatever form. The same is true with a set as well as with measurement. Conservation, therefore, is a fundamental process underlying rational thought and hence is at the root of scientific inquiry.

In terms of a developmental order, during the period from birth to two years of age, the prerequisite to conservation, *object permanence,* is established. Object permanence refers to knowing that the existence of something remains, irrespective of whether it is perceivable (i.e., the baby comes to realize that "mother" does not cease to exist just because she leaves the bedroom where the baby is).

Object permanence is followed by perceptual *constancy—* knowing that the identity of something remains the same irrespective of the particular perspective from which it is being perceived. As an example, a saucer, which is round, may look cigar-shaped when viewed at an angle. However, we know that from the top view its roundness remains the same even though it looks cigar-shaped when we look at it from a different perspective. During the preoperational period, ages three to seven years approximately, the child comes to first understand qualitative consistencies, followed by the understanding of quantitative invariance concerning number, length, mass or substance, area, and continuous quantity.

Math educators have long recognized that grasping the basic meaning of number should precede representation using symbols. Otherwise, the child will be either confused or will memorize answers by rote rather than attain a fundamental understanding. Grasping the meaning of number relations depends on the child's ability to understand the quantitative attribute of a set of items, which involves classification; to understand the asymmetrical relationship between those items based on their recognized differences, which involves seriation; to make quantitative inferences on the basis of equivalences and differences, which involves transitivity; and to understand that the identity of the quantitative attributes as they are classified remains constant, which involves conservation. The child's ability to perform logical operations or processes is evidence of the existence of those psychological structures for ascertaining the meaning underlying quantitative relationships.

There may be other cognitive processes not yet identified which are basic to a child's understanding of number relations. Much more theoretical work is required coupled with longitudinal empirical research to determine if this is so. Because of the amount of research done to date, it is unlikely that the processes mentioned in this paper will take on less significance. Rather, I would expect that further research will make more formidable the argument justifying their inclusion in the curriculum, and continued and detailed study of each will yield for educators more useful information about their characteristics and how their development can be fostered in children.

We've come a long way in both identifying and redressing the weaknesses in both traditional and modern math programs. However, we have not arrived, nor shall we arrive easily, at the point of having the ideal math program given human proclivity to create potential, thus continuing to evolve. The task which remains is to find out in great detail how a child comes to understand number relationships. Our method is theory construction based on what we know about how people learn, the application of theory to curriculum development and teaching, and empirical verification of the theory.

References

Ausubel, D.P. "The Transition from Concrete to Abstract Cognitive Functioning: Theoretical Issues and Implications." In *Educational Implications of Piaget's Theory,* edited by I.J. Athey and D.O. Rubadean. Waltham, Mass.: Ginn-Blaisdell, 1970.

Boyle, D.G. *A Student's Guide to Piaget.* Oxford, England: Pergamon Press, 1969.

Bruner, J.S.; Goodnow, J.J.; and Austin, G.A. *A Study of Thinking.* New York: John Wiley and Sons, 1956.

Kline, M. *Why Johnny Can't Add: The Failure of the New Math.* New York: St. Martin's Press, 1973.

Lovell, K. "The Growth of Understanding in Mathematics: Kindergarten Through Grade Three." *Early Childhood Education Series.* New York: Holt, Rinehart, and Winston, 1971.

Piaget, J. *The Child's Conception of Number.* New York: W.W. Norton & Co., 1965.

Raman, S.P. "Role of Nutrition in the Actualization of the Potentialities of the Child: An Anisa Perspective." *Young Children* 31, no.1 (November 1975): 24-32.

Rosskopf, M.F.; Steffe, L.P.; and Taback, S., eds. *Piagetian Cognitive Development Research and Mathematical Education.* Reston, Va.: National Council of Teachers of Mathematics, 1971.

Stern, C., and Stern, M.B. *Children Discover Arithmetic: An Introduction to Structural Arithmetic.* New York: Harper and Row, Publishers, 1971.

Whitehead, A.N. *Science and Philosophy.* Patterson, N.J.: Littlefield, Adams and Co., 1964.

Bilingual/ Bicultural Education: Separating Facts from Fiction

George A. González, *Director, Bilingual Bicultural Studies Program, Pan American University, Edinburg, Texas.*

Education is supported as a science by those who maintain that it is composed of a series of predictable and exact phenomena, both visible and measurable, and that these manifestations can be regularized and managed. The scientific view of education would propose the existence of a theory operationalized through a consistent set of hypotheses, strategies, and media. The teacher would tend to favor a technical and objective approach in preparation and instruction.

Education can be conversely explained as an art by those who maintain that it is composed of a series of inspirational and incidental phenomena, both subjective and imprecise, and that these manifestations are usually spontaneous and flexible. The artistic view of education would propose the existence of a gifted spirit seen through a process of intuition, action, and media. The teacher would tend to favor an open and subjective approach in preparation and instruction.

I would like to present a few thoughts about bilingual/bicultural education: dealing with it not as a science, nor as an art, but rather examining a dimension somewhere between the objectivity of science and the subjectivity of art. And that is the area of myths in education.

Early peoples invented

93

myths in order to help explain that which they could not understand or that which they feared. Today in our schools bilingual/bicultural education is often fraught with vague misconceptions, unfounded judgments, and half truths. We in education must make an effort to understand more clearly and perhaps begin to appreciate the validity of this most innovative concept as an alternative in the education of children with linguistic and cultural differences.

The young boy, who in Albuquerque's bilingual education program attempted to enter a girl's rest room, was met by an anxious teacher reprimanding the child: "Juan, why are you going into the girl's rest room?" The boy quickly responded in surprise: "I thought this was a bilingual school!" Vague misconceptions, unfounded judgments, half truths, ...

The English-speaking lady who recently visited the Rio Grande Valley of Texas questioned the quality of Spanish spoken locally as not quite Castilian, which she had learned at the university. Upon hearing an English-speaking priest celebrate a Spanish language wedding in a heavy English-accented manner: "Estamos aquí para celebrar la boda de estos dos jóvenes . . . ." She was heard exclaiming: "At last, I've heard Castilian Spanish!" Vague misconceptions, unfounded judgments, half truths, ...

The educator who was heard inquiring of the Spanish language: "You mean that in Spanish you can think? You can say things like 'cognitive domain' and 'Bloom's taxonomy'?" And I answer: "Naturalmente, decimos 'dominio cognoscitivo' y 'la taxonomía de Bloom'." Vague misconceptions, unfounded judgments, and half truths, ...

The little old lady who in protesting a speaker's comments about bilingual/bicultural education, remarked: "Young man, you are threatening the very fabric of American society." Unfounded judgments, vague misconceptions, half truths, ...

Bilingual education is thus regarded by many as controversial, confusing, and complex. Controversial, because to many it threatens the basic melting-pot mold of an American who speaks only English, values one style of life, and practices the behaviors of the middle-class White society. Confusing, to those who are expecting one universal bilingual/bicultural education model practiced throughout the country and are confused in finding that there may be as many variations in bilingual/bicultural education as there are programs. And complex, because as we attempt to define a quality education experience for children through a "dual language" system within a bicultural setting, the number of variables to deal with are innumerable.

Following will be presented twenty statements which I maintain are myths in American education. The first set of five myths address themselves to general education. The remaining fifteen myths focus on language, culture, and instruction in the field of bilingual/bicultural education.

I. MYTHS IN GENERAL EDUCATION

These are five myths which I suggest apply to the education of all young children; myths that have been perpetrated and maintained by the educational systems in the country, especially by the institutions of higher learning where professors of education recommend that teachers should:

A. Meet the needs, interests, and abilities of students.

This obviously is based on the theory that schools should serve children and that the curriculum should be developed around children's characteristics. Because children naturally are our most prized resource, and rather than change children to serve the schools, the school would serve the needs of children. I suggest this as one of the myths in general education because of the prevalence of situations such as the following:

The teacher issues the directive: "Today, children, we will conjugate the present subjunctive verbs in their first person plural form." And that being of very little interest to children, we find them in various occupations as the teacher "does his thing" (Fig. 1).

Figure 1

Myth number two: We have been told for many generations by the institutions of higher education to:

B. Consider individual differences.

because we know that each individual has unique and personal attributes which make that person a distinct member of the group. It is a very sound theory, but what we find in practice is the teacher talking to the multitudes saying, "Let's all turn to page 33 and do 15 problems for tomorrow."

Myth number three. We have also been told:

C. Start where the child is, and take him as far as possible.

We have been told that early behavior and learning is important; that the background of experience of the child is crucial; that the child's frame of reference, initial and previous concepts and skills are essential in advancing cognitive, linguistic, and psychomotor competencies. And what we find in schools many times is the teacher reprimanding the child with: "You're asking about something which was covered last year. *Sorry,* we"ll just have to go on . . . . "

The fourth myth in general education tells us that you:

D. Go from the known to the unknown.

How often we have heard this statement! One must begin with learned and familiar materials and proceed gradually, building on what has already been gained. You are to use what the child has learned as the basis for new learning experiences. Many times, what the child faces, though, is going from one set of unknowns and confronting another set of unknowns while crossing the bridge into new learning. And we continue to teach from the unknown . . . to the unknown . . . to the unknown.

The last of the five myths in general education is:

E. Teach the complete child.

Teach the complete child: We are not to ignore each child's academic, social, cultural, economic, emotional, physiological, nor linguistic characteristics. We are not to ignore any of these inherent elements when we plan a curriculum. What we often find is the teacher accepting the child into the classroom by allowing only part to enter—that

Figure 2

part which is English—and omitting his culture, language, and home (Fig. 2).

Those are the five myths that I maintain operate in much of what we do in general education. I would like to proceed now and present myths which deal with bilingual/bicultural education.

II. MYTHS ABOUT BILINGUAL/BICULTURAL EDUCATION.

We have been involved in bilingual/bicultural education now for approximately ten years. Because there has been confusion due to the complexity and the controversy mentioned earlier, and because people fear and mistrust innovative concepts exploring new frontiers, often educators have built around them a set of myths.

A. LANGUAGE

The first which deals with language is as follows:

1. The Spanish dialect of the Southwest is not really a language: therefore, it is not worthy of study and maintenance. Proper and correct Spanish can only be found in those who speak Castilian Spanish.

I have found many teachers who claim: "We do try to teach these children through Spanish, but I learned Castilian Spanish at the University, and I can't understand what they're saying." I maintain that if Castilian Spanish is the language that we are to prize, then we in Texas have to begin to prize British-English, and British-English must then be the norm for the kind of English we speak in Texas. To the same degree that Texas-English is considered a worthy dialect of English or a proper variety of English, so must the dialect of Spanish in Texas be considered a worthy and a beautiful version of the Spanish language.

What we might find otherwise is the ridiculous situation of Mexican-Americans imitating the Spaniards in saying: "No hay *th*ielo tan *ath*ul como el *th*ielo de andalu*th*ia. ¿No cree, Señor?" And, the Americans responding in proper British tones: "I do believe you're right, old chap, except for that beastly fortnight when the rain fell mainly on the plain."

The second myth in language is:

2. The English language should be the initial learning vehicle for all children in school regardless of their language background.

This has its roots in our ethnocentric spirit in this country, as we seem to believe that the English language is the only language through which a person could conceptualize. How could anybody think in any other language except the English language? Even God communicates with the angels in English!

So if we believe that true abstract conceptualizations at the highest cognitive level can only be achieved through the English language, we, then, find situations in our schools where the teacher says:

"Children, will you please rise and we will attend to our class opening exercises. We will first recite the pledge, then we will check the roll, and then . . . . " And the children say: "¿Qué dijo? ¡Quién sabe!"

The third of the language myths:

3. **A standard accent and intonation is to be considered a mark of the educated and the intelligent; those with a detectable foreign accent in their speech are to be considered comical, alien, or ignorant.**

So we have situations where we hear Chevalier speak and we say: "Oh, those French are so romantic! They say 'take out the garbage' in French . . . and it sounds so *romantic.* Zsa Zsa Gabor—she sounds so glamorous . . . she's so sexy . . . . " We look to people like our friend Henry who says: "Vell, vunce more we hab peace in the vorld" (Fig. 3). And we say: "How brilliant! How well-organized! . . . What a marvelous intellect!"

What kind of conception do *you* have about a person who speaks English with a Spanish accent?

Figure 3

Number four:

4. The Spanish language is limited as a teaching vehicle in the transmission of concepts and principles.

We give testimony to the fact that it *is* possible to transmit concepts through the following scene: a situation where a man says, "Este *yip* necesita un *mofle,* un *clotche,* y la *spare* and a *flat.*" And the man responds, "Fix it *pronto* because I have to get to the *corral* and *lasso* my *pinto.* We're gonna go to the *rodeo*!" So that, indeed, we *can* borrow from the English into our Spanish; and we can borrow from the Spanish into English. And, thus, become quite effective in transmitting concepts and principles.

The last of the language myths:

5. These Mexican-American children are not really bilingual. They do not speak English or Spanish; they are nonlingual.

How can children be nonlingual, if they *are* expressing themselves in some form? Do they perhaps communicate with their toes? Children certainly employ a form of verbal and nonverbal language in a scene such as: "Yo quiero de *Santa Clos* un *doll* muy *pretty* y muchos *dishes.*" And another child answers, "Para *Crismas I want* un carro *red* y una *big bicycle.*" We *can* communicate. We are bilingual. We *are not* nonlingual. Those are the language myths. I proceed now with the culture myths.

B. CULTURE

We find groups who came from Norway, from England, from Scotland who say:

1. If we could give up our culture, why not them?

"Why must they maintain their strange language and strange ways. We gave up our culture. Why aren't they willing to give up their culture?" We have to respond: "Is this process necessarily so? Do we all have to fit one mold? Is the melting-pot concept really operating? Must we all go through the same Americanization process?" (Fig. 4). All the different ethnic groups as they go through this process exit

Figure 4

from this machine—out of this process—looking identical. Must we all look like Dick and Jane to be American? Can we be allowed some of our differences? Can we speak a different language, and English also? Can we eat different foods and hold different values and still be considered as American as apple pie and as American as *empanadas*?

The second myth in culture is promoted by many prominent Mexican-Americans—the Mexican-American who has "made it."

2. If we could make it in the system, why not them?

This guy has a Ph.D., he's got a D.P.T., and X.Y.Z., and A.B.C.; he's got all kinds of degrees. And he feels he's made it. He says: "How come if I could make it, why can't they make it?" And you observe the following scene where the Mexican-American portrays the "Super-Anglo" . . . in his bathrobe, his slippers, by the fireplace, sipping a martini, a huge dog . . . saying: "I made it, why can't they?"

The next myth some people contend is:

3. It's un-American!

"It is not 'American' to want to speak Spanish," they claim. Some people in the southern part of Texas go as far as to say: "Ship them back to Mexico . . . deport them . . . put them in buses . . . send them back! If they want to speak Spanish, they have got to realize that in this country, *that* is not valued." So, bilingual/bicultural education in some quarters is considered "un-American."

The established misconceptions and half-truths create the fear that:

4. They're trying to make Mexicans of us all.

The belief is that the bilingual education movement seeks identity with Mexico, pledging allegiance to the Mexican flag, obeying the Mexican Constitution and the Mexican president . . . . That is as far away from the truth as possible.

In the use of objects and behaviors from Mexico is the value system which perhaps began in Mexico, but these traditions should be considered Americana of the Southwest and not allegiance to the Republic of Mexico.

The fifth of the culture myths seems positive and harmless as some will claim:

5. There are more cultural similarities than there are differences.

"We are all more alike than we are different. Why do we keep emphasizing the differences? We're all basically the *same*. Let's behave as human beings with common characteristics and let's not emphasize the differences." I agree that there are certainly many similarities. All the various groups enjoy eating, resting, working, traveling, and all the good things in life. These are the commonalities, but they are not the problem areas which cause distress and frustration. The areas that create the problems are the differences. It is the small differences that at times explode into problems. Examine the typical American scene as the woman enters and says: "I made some sandwiches for a snack." It is a very ordinary event. Yet another scene is also similar: The woman comes in and says, "Les hice unos taquitos para merendar."

There are many commonalities here between the two scenes. But the language is different, and one finds that diet can also be different. These differences which sometimes cause problems need to be examined and studied. They need at least to be considered in our curriculum for young children.

C. INSTRUCTION

The last set of myths deal with instruction—the area of basic teaching strategies.

Sometimes we erroneously say that:

1. The methodology best suited to teach the Mexican-American a second language is found in a structured and sequential oral language program dependent on drill and repetition.

And after having established this myth, we tie ourselves to one methodology that is direct and structured, based on drills and repetition—oftentimes monotonous experiences. Picture the following scene: "Pedro, make a sentence with the word *was*." The boy responds, "The was can run." With little understanding of what he is saying, he mimics and parrots words (Fig. 5).

The opposite of this previous myth claims that:

Figure 5

2. The methodology best suited to teach the Mexican-American a second language is found in a nonstructured and open-ended language program dependent on incidental and situational learning.

If we go too far in the other direction, I think we are creating a myth about instruction as haphazard and chaotic. As a result one may find situations such as the following in which the teacher is saying: "Look, class, look what José brought to school today. Tell us about it José so we can have a lesson on it." And the boy says, "Well, my mother was *ragging* the flowers and I saw this big *ran* and I catch it to brought to you, Miss." "Ragging," for those who don't understand, is an Anglicism formed from the verb *regar* (to water the plants), therefore, *ragging.* And "ran" comes from *rana*, the frog (Fig. 6).

Sometimes, instruction becomes so accidental and unstructured that the children fail to learn grammaticality of sentences—the structure of speech—and lose, then, to a degree, a sense of communication. Somewhere between these two opposing myths, we need to find an adequate middle ground.

The third of the instructional myths:

3. Any Spanish speaking adult is automatically competent in the field of instruction of young children whose first language is also Spanish.

In other words, "If the adult speaks Spanish, just take her out of the community, bring her into the classroom, and she is automatically competent to teach young children. As long as she speaks Spanish, she can be made responsible for the Spanish instructional component in bilingual/bicultural education." Language cannot be considered the only competency or ability needed in the instructicn of young children in Spanish. The illustration (Fig. 7) depicts a classroom setting in which the teacher says: "Síganle, síganle, bola de salvajes. Si no se ponen a trabajar en el *workbook* van a ver lo que les va a pasar!" One can hurt and damage children in the Spanish language as effectively as through the English language.

The fourth of the instructional myths:

4. In bilingual education, one simply adds a Spanish component to the existing curriculum and instruction.

Figure 6

Figure 7

This is certainly one of the most damaging myths. In other words, this misconception develops the notion that all one has to do is continue the same "garbage" that we have been doing for the last thirty, forty, fifty years with children who are linguistically and culturally different. Take the same practices, translate them into Spanish, carry them out in English in the morning and in Spanish in the afternoon—and that's supposed to pass for bilingual education.

We must not merely translate the experiences and the activities that we have been using in the past into Spanish and label it a bilingual/bicultural education program. If we are to continue hurting children in school, leave the Spanish for the home.

An illustration might be a cook preparing an alphabet soup in English. He then adds the "ñ", the "ll", and the "ch" and assumes he's cooking a bilingual *caldo,* or soup. The process of developing a valid bilingual/bicultural education program is much more complex and difficult that this.

The last of the instruction myths maintains that

5. The Spanish component of a bilingual instructional program can be delegated to a paraprofessional aide in the classroom.

In other words, "If the teacher is monolingual English-speaking, all one has to do is turn over the Spanish instruction to the teacher aide. This is sufficient in the development of a bilingual program."

The aide many times is not competently trained. The children see the dominant person in the classroom, the teacher, as "la patrona" or the "jefe." The leader speaks English and the subservient underling takes care of the Spanish. This practice could gradually depict to young children, then, that English is dominant and Spanish subservient.

We, as professionals, must learn the language of the child or delegate it to another professional who already knows the language, but never assign it entirely to the teacher aide. Although teacher aides can contribute much to the instructional program, we cannot totally delegate the Spanish portion of the bilingual program to paraprofessionals. In the illustration (Fig. 8) we face a situation where the English-speaking teacher is comfortably teaching at the blackboard while the untrained teacher aide is attempting: "Hoy vamos a estudiar ... ah ... estudiar ... ah ...." And she may not know how to proceed, how to present a concept, how to present a skill. She may not know a taxonomy of intellectual sequences. Therefore, many times one may do damage to children who are not guided properly by a trained professional.

III. THE ONE MAJOR MYTH

In presenting the last myth, the big myth, the one major myth, the super myth, . . . it is believed that:

Bilingual education can succeed by merely implementing the same traditional process through a two language system.

This reiterates one of the previous myths, but I want to highlight it as perhaps the most damaging of the myths. If one follows the same traditional practices, if the quality of interaction between the child and

Figure 8

teacher has not changed, if we continue to follow the same organizational patterns of instruction, if we insist on assigning students the same mindless kinds of tasks under the guise of bilingual/bicultural education, I maintain it can be very damaging.

If one believes that all one does is translate the practices of yesteryear into Spanish and suddenly one has developed a bilingual education program, this is a *myth*.

We have to review the entire process: consider the linguistic and cultural characteristics of children and build from the bottom a program that talks about *quality education* through a bilingual mode within a bicultural setting—an environment in which children are truly inspired to conceptualize at high abstract levels cognitively and bilingually.

I would like to finish with my one bilingual joke. Everybody in South Texas has heard it . . . custodians, teachers, nurses, principals, superintendents . . . . I am attempting (and I know it's an ambitious undertaking) to make it the "national bilingual joke." I hope that during the Bicentennial it receives recognition as the bilingual/bicultural Bicentennial joke. (You need to be bilingual to appreciate it.)

It seems that in San Antonio, Texas, there is an area in the West Side that was considered by St. Teresa up in heaven as deprived, awfully deprived. And St. Teresa, in her wisdom, knowing the value of being "American" and speaking English (and only speaking English), realized that these deprived (depraved) Mexican-Americans in the barrio of the West Side needed to learn to speak English and to abandon the silly language called "Spanish," because they must be "American"; and the only way to be "American" is to speak "American." So she convinced St. Peter that they must write a federal proposal to submit to Washington, and she would then receive these funds and go down in the barrio to work for one year, totally erradicating the Spanish language from the West Side. She wrote it, complete with behavioral objectives; she received the funds; she went to the barrio; she worked diligently, like only a saint could work for one entire year.

She went back to heaven and reported, "I'm sorry, I was unable to fulfill the entire mission. We are beginning to understand these people and . . . well let's get the thing refunded." She said, "I ask for six months. I think I can wrap it up in six months." They got the project refunded; she spent six months working laboriously, untiringly. She worked even more than before.

After the six months, she went back and said, "I am very sorry, but I have once more failed to convert these Mexicans to follow the true and the only 'way'; but we have some money left over in the parental involvement component." (There's always money left over there.) She said, "If I were allowed to go down there three more months, I think I can accomplish my mission because I now know what makes them tick. I understand them, and I think I can wipe them out." She went back to San Antonio. She worked the three months; went back to heaven; knocks at the gates of heaven . . . no response . . . she knocks again . . . no response . . . she knocks again . . . still no response . . . and you hear her voice call out to St. Peter:

"Ésele Pete, ábrame la portacha, no sea gacho. Ésta es la *Terry* . . . " She is now the patron saint of bilingual education. If you want a proposal funded, you pray to her. It really works!

Should the Public Schools Control Child Care Services?

(Part I)

A Panel Presentation

Barbara Bowman, *Director, Erikson Institute for Early Education, Chicago, Illinois.*

Barbara Bowman and Eugenia Kemble, members of a panel which considered the question "Should the Public Schools Control Child Care Services?", discuss some of the vital issues surrounding this question from two viewpoints.

I would like to begin by explaining that I have two separate statements to make. One is a resolution submitted by the Boards of the Chicago and Illinois Associations for the Education of Young Children to the NAEYC membership meeting at this conference in respect to the sponsorship of a comprehensive child care bill. In the second statement I would like to explain briefly why I voted for this resolution. It is important to note that the second statment is my own and does not necessarily reflect the position of the members of either of the two boards. I particularly want to credit Lynn Pooley, Michael Phair, and Judi McWilliams for the work they did in preparing the resolutions for the joint CAEYC-IAEYC Legislative Task Force.

The resolution, as amended and passed at the NAEYC membership meeting on November 14, 1975, reads:

> WHEREAS Comprehensive Child Care Legislation, S. 626 and H.R. 2966, has been introduced in Congress; and WHEREAS there is con-

111

troversy over who should be named "prime sponsor" if such legislation is passed; and WHEREAS the Mondale-Brademas Bill* of 1975 is written to allow any single qualified agency to be considered for prime sponsorship as opposed limiting sponsorship to only one specified category;

THEREFORE BE IT RESOLVED that the National Association for the Education of Young Children

    1. *Endorse the concept of allowing many eligible groups to be considered for the prime sponsorship of services to children through national legislation, as provided in Bill S. 626 and H.R. 2966,*

    2. *Urge all Affiliate Groups to mobilize support in their own communities to insure Presidential approval of the Bill, and*

    3. *Forward copies of this resolution to all members of Congress, the Secretary of Health, Education, and Welfare, and the Director of the Office of Child Development.*

Submitted by the Boards of the Illinois Association for the Education of Young Children and the Chicago Association for the Education of Young Children

Now , my own statement:

In August of 1974, Senator Walter Mondale and Representative John Brademas introduced the newest version of a comprehensive child care bill entitled Child and Family Services Act of 1975 (S. 626 and H.R. 2966 in the 1976 legislative session). The bill itself has drawn comparatively little comment: the proposed amendments to the bill put forth by the American Federation of Teachers (AFT) have raised a furor. In particular, AFT President Albert Shanker has called for amending the bill to provide for prime sponsorship of the child care program by the public schools.

The rationale for this administrative design has several essential points. First, it is an employment program for the current oversup-

---

*The Child and Family Services Act

ply of teachers. Eugenia Kemble (1975) says, "By defining day care in educational terms, and by relating its expansion to current conditions in the public schools, the AFT has attempted to combine the interests of children with the interests of its members" (p. 1). While the forthright advertisement of "self-interest" on the part of the school union has offended a large section of the early childhood community, this is certainly not the first time that programs for young children have been used to provide vocational opportunities for adults. Sears and Dowley (1963) comment:

> . . .throughout the history of nursery education in the United States, the primary objective of the nursery schools has often been the welfare of persons other than the children. Preparental education of high school and college students, teacher training, and research have been added to parent education, teacher employment, and the provision of custodial care for children of employed mothers as the main objectives of the nursery schools. (p. 815)

Since these words were written, a variety of employment related programs in the field of child care have been proposed and enacted. OEO, CDA, the Long amendment, CETA, and Mainstream (to name a few) have joined WPA and Lanham Act Nurseries as measures designed to provide for the economic needs of adults and young children in the same package.

The fact that the AFT proposal is an employment plan for teachers should not prejudice us against it. The critical question we must ask about the AFT proposal is whether this latest employment plan will prove beneficial to young children and their families, for I am sure that all of us, including the AFT, do not wish to initiate programs which will work against the best interests of our children.

What kind of information do we have about the impact of employment plans on early childhood programs and the children enrolled in these programs? We have some suggestions from a number of Head Start and other intervention models that proverty's children achieve better in communities steadied by jobs and training in child development. That is, long-term changes in the lives of children are more reliably attained when we can change the lives of their parents and the meaningful others in their communities. Economic stability and parent education are important adjuncts to the classroom education of many of our children. It is on this score that the AFT proposal is found wanting, for their proposal would, in effect, render ineligible a segment of the community—poor people who are currently receiving both financial benefits and training through federally funded programs. Instead, the money and training would be largely taken away from the poverty community to be given to the middle class certified teacher. Even where opportunities exist in public schools, as in the teacher aide position, the monetary reward and vocational opportunity are considerably diminished.

Are there any advantages to employment of certified teachers to offset the loss of money and education to poor parents and community folk? The advantage most frequently cited is that the certified teacher is better able to plan and implement programs for young children because of teacher college education and as evidenced by having passed a teacher examination.

We have little or no evidence to support this position. Most certified elementary teachers are paraprofessionals in early childhood education. They must learn to work with the young child and they must learn to work with the child's parents. It is necessary to retrain public school teachers just as it is necessary to train the noncertified teacher.

Another aspect of the AFT plan that we must consider goes under the rubric of "crises in confidence." By this, I refer to the fact that in many communities the school is failing. One has only to pass the boarded up windows, read the statistics on teacher attacks, and check out achievement scores to be aware that all is not well in many of our public schools. It is not our task here today to discuss why it is true that for many of our people the public school has lost its credibility and responsiveness. It is sufficient for us to recognize that where this is the case the school does not make the ideal support system for young children and their families. Where the public schools are not viewed as partners in the achievement of a family's aspirations, then it is foolhardy to entrust it with the delivery of a child and family support service.

This should not be taken to mean that public schools always do an inadequate job working with poor and minority people. In some communities, for some people, the school has indeed provided quality programs and should be encouraged to continue with these fine programs and to develop new ones. But poor and minority communities cannot afford to trust the benevolence of any one institution. They cannot trust that they will receive the necessary education from the public schools to thrust them out of the morass of racism, victimization, and paternalism.

Mr. Shanker recommends that where prejudice and discrimination pertain and the public schools in a White district do not choose to service Black children, the government could intervene (Auerbach 1975, p. 9). It is not our fear in the Black community that programs will not be provided, but rather that the kinds of programs provided will not serve the best interests of our children. Schools may not be relied upon by the poor and minorities to deliver needed services to their *young children* in any more creditable a fashion than they have delivered services to their older children. We must not put all of our early childhood eggs in the same basket.

In my mind another deterrent to exclusive sponsorship of child care programs must clearly be the inflexibility and rigidity that afflicts large administrative units including public schools. The centralized bureaucracies have considerable difficulty in responding to diverse needs, to changing conditions, and to new visions for the future. Although we have many individual examples of the creativity and innovation that is possible within the public school system, we also have considerable evidence that the large systems are beset with problems of wages and hours, role definitions, standardized treatments, etc. These bureacratic concerns all too frequently add up to constriction and complacency.

Our knowledge about what and how children are best taught during the first six years is vast, but it is still far from sufficient. We do not know all of the conditions necessary to rear humane, thoughtful, creative people. It is a mistake, therefore, to standardize and lockstep a curriculum. Just as we offer the opportunity for individual children to march to the tune of a different drummer, so too must we preserve the opportunity for different programs and teachers to discover and promote a variety of different curricula. I believe we maximize creativity and innovation by encouraging a variety of program designs and competition for excellence. Alternative strategies for teacher education and credentialing, alternatives in curriculum content and methodology, diversity in family-centered/school relationships, deficiencies in length of school day, all seem more easily achieved when administered by different agencies. I am opposed to prime sponsorship in the hands of any one service-delivering agency. Far better, I think, to allocate the money through a state agency whose primary responsibility is not the direct delivery of child care and education.

I would like to add, however, that many of the problems noted by the AFT are valid and appropriate criticism of the current child care scene. These include poor quality of physical plant, unhealthy and unsafe environments, inadequate staff, low standards for licensing, and, most important, refusal to recognize the educational importance of early childhood years. If delegation of the program to the public school is not the answer, what is?

I believe, with the AFT, that we need an extension of child care and education benefits. The provision of separate school systems for

Black and White children has been found to be inherently discriminatory. Separate schools for the rich and the poor are also inherently discriminatory. As long as there are schools exclusively for the poor we will undoubtedly continue the pattern of unreliable funding, capricious rules and regulations, paternalistic attitudes, and irrelevant demands on parents and children so familiar in Head Start and Title programs.

The need of working mothers for quality child care is as pertinent in the middle class as it is to the poor. And the ability to pay for quality care is almost as seriously compromised. We must be willing to support cost subsidies if the middle class is to also have decent child care and education.

In addition, there are middle class families where mother does not work but where there is a need for preschool programs. These children and families must be a part of our preschool package just as are families served by Head Start and day care.

I agree also with the AFT that we need a unified constituency to work for more and better child care. But a unified constituency which includes *not only* the public schools but also church-related, community-based, and privately-funded program personnel. A constituency that is made up of parents as well as teachers, of poor and middle classes, of Black and White, urban and rural. A constituency made up of all who recognize the importance of our children.

I hope that NAEYC will be a part of that constituency.

I hope you all will be!

References

Auerbach, S. "An Interview with Albert Shanker." *Day Care and Early Education,* September/October 1975.

Kemble, E. "Starting Off on the Right Foot." *The American Teacher,* Magazine Section, March 1975.

Sears, P., and Dowley, E. "Research on Training in the Nursery School." In *Handbook on Research on Teaching,* edited by N.L. Nage. Chicago: Rand, McNally and Co., 1963.

Should the Public Schools Control Child Care Services?

(Part II)

A Panel Presentation

Eugenia Kemble, *Special Assistant to the President of the American Federation of Teachers, Washington, D.C.*

Barbara Bowman and Eugenia Kemble, members of a panel which considered the question "Should the Public Schools Control Child Care Services?", discuss some of the vital issues surrounding this question from two viewpoints.

The question of the control of child care services is really very closely tied to the kinds of needs this country now has for good day care, as well as our notions of what a quality program should be. We do not believe these issues can be separated. Unfortunately, the kind of position the American Federation of Teachers has taken on the issue of public school sponsorship is often featured by others as a power grab. I would urge you to look closely at the arguments I am going to make about control as it relates to program needs and program quality. I also ask that you consider the role organizations like yours and mine play vis-à-vis the day care question with these arguments in mind.

There are a lot of very clear and convincing reasons being presented now for expanding day care and early childhood services in this country. But, before I go into them I just want to remind you that as convincing as the needs arguments are, we do not *yet* have a comprehensive national program. Richard Nixon vetoed the

119

Child Development Title of the Economic Opportunity Act in 1971. President Ford has already said that he will veto the Child and Family Services Act (S. 626 and H.R. 2966 in the 1976 legislative session) being considered by House and Senate Committees. I understand that the kind of opposition to day care that views it as a threat to motherhood and the family is mounting a powerful fight to kill the present bill. This means that the way we go about working to obtain the kind of national program we want needs to be examined very carefully. I hope you will consider our failures to date in the light of what I have to say.

First, I will assume all of you have heard a lot of statistics reflecting the needs of working women for day care services. I will also assume that these statistics are pretty convincing and that this is not an issue about which we need to have much discussion. In looking at this whole area we must also consider (1) mothers who would work if they could and (2) single men or women who would work if they could or (3) those who do work, leaving their children unsupervised—and with unhappy consequences. Most of you have probably heard the term "latch-key children." Senator Mondale pointed out in his introductory statement on the Child and Family Services Bill that there are only about one million spaces available in licensed day care programs for preschool children whose mothers are working. He also noted that between 1970 and 1973 there was an increase of 650,000 in the number of children whose mothers work. In 1973, six million children under six years old had mothers who were working or looking for work. According to the best estimates, there are now four million day care slots and only one million of these are licensed.

Second, I am also pretty sure that we are in agreement about the importance of the early years to the growth and development of children. I am not going to get into a long discussion on how much of a child's intellectual development takes place at certain ages, but there certainly is plenty of evidence to indicate that the preschool years are crucial. As educators of young children you know very well that they need to be stimulated at this time; they need to be encouraged; they need exposure to materials that will excite their curiosity and thinking. All homes do not provide these things—whether for reasons of poverty, ignorance, or availability. Nor are they provided by much of what now constitutes day care—but I will get to that later.

These are the needs of children and families at the most basic level. Acceptance of the merits of these arguments, it seems to me, points to another set of needs which people interested in providing these services simply must look at. These needs have to do with the quality of program.

1. The American Federation of Teachers (AFT) believes, given the importance of the early years, that day care and early childhood programs must be more than custodial operations. If children are to get the stimulation they need, comprehensive programs must provide such services as early diagnosis, guidance counseling, health services, bilingual education, education for the handicapped, and dieticians, as well as programs to stimulate intellectual development.

2. We also think that good day care and early childhood education need to reflect the quality that comes only from the application of standards; the present situation does not provide for this—either by way of certification for early childhood experts at the level of preschool, building codes and regulations, child-staff ratios, etc.

3. The AFT maintains that programs such as these must be really *free, universal,* and *voluntary.* These ideas are really central to our whole analysis of the *needs* in this area. If some of those who differ with us would take a good look at these concepts I think they would understand better where we are coming from. Let me spell this out:

   a. These programs should be free so that everyone who wants them—for whatever reasons—can take advantage of them. They should not be tied to restrictive means tests—which may lead to segregation of programs, narrow constituencies, and the lack of broad-based support for their continuation.

   b. Universality relates to the nature of potential support for these programs too. First of all, the quality of the programs is likely to be better if many different kinds of children—income-wise and culture-wise—are in them. It is also more likely that they will generate more widespread public interest and support. It is also only fair that everyone have the opportunity to avail themselves of the programs supported with federal funds. Some will say that this is basically a political argument. In part it is. All we need to do is look at the history of day care legislation in this country to understand why worrying about breadth of support is important, hence: universality. In short, we do not want to split off day care from the rest of education and thereby isolate it.

c. We believe these programs must be voluntary because they are intended for children of very young ages. Many parents want to stay home and raise their children themselves during these crucial years. This should be their choice.

4. I might also say here that we do not think that what is needed is a whole new bureaucracy to administer such programs—a charge which has been leveled at the AFT. We maintain that the administering apparatus exists in the public school system, and that it should be used. There already are certification and licensing mechanisms, building codes, etc., that should be used.

So far I have addressed myself to the AFT's view of what the needs are. Obviously they are an outgrowth of our interpretation of what the problems are in day care and early childhood programs.

First, I want to emphasize that there are some good child care and early education programs in existence. Many of them are out of reach of the average parent for some of the reasons I have cited. Others, including some of those now publicly funded, are not so good. There is much documentation to support the claim that day care is in large part inadequate. Let me cite a few examples:

1. The well-known report published by the National Council of Jewish Women called *Windows on Day Care* (1972) found that all the centers in the proprietary category provided service that was essentially custodial. Half of those observed were regarded as poor. Note: A recent Census Bureau report (1974) states that about three-

fourths of nursery school enrollment is in private schools, so the inadequacy of private care is really a serious issue.

2. Nonprofit centers are somewhat better than the profit makers. The *Windows on Day Care* report found half of these to be "fair," though only about one-quarter of them met the "good" standard set in the report. *Early Schooling in the United States* (1973) is another report which found most of the day care centers observed to be inadequate in terms of numbers of kinds of activities and general program quality. The researchers attributed the quality of the lesser programs to the fact that they were not a part of the public school system and hence not exposed to mainstream arguments and discussions about education.

3. Lack of funds: the failure of states to provide matching grants for federal funds.

4. The critical reports I have cited put much of the blame for poor program quality on states which set low staff qualifications and have, for the most part, inadequate licensing provisions. Certification requirements in some states are often as low as "equipped for work required," whatever that means. The picture is made clear by a recent HEW audit (1974) which says that of 552 centers and private day care homes in nine states, 425 did not meet minimum health and safety requirements and over one-third did not meet child/staff ratio requirements. The report attributed such failing to jurisdictional confusion and overlap in administrative responsibility.

For me to make these criticisms may seem like a very tough approach to take. Yet, for all the talk about lack of flexibility and all of the concern over public school bureaucracy, such analyses of the current state of day care cannot be ignored—there are real problems. And, though the public schools themselves have problems, I think it is safe to say that day care has more. As I said before, this kind of assessment of what our needs are and this grim picture of the problems have led us to the particular view of the control issue that we have come to. In saying this I don't mean to imply that the self-interest of our members who are looking for jobs is not a factor. It is. But any social program that is worth anything involves responding to interests. We think this one presents a good response to the combined interests of parents, teachers, and children.

The next thing I want to look at is the present act before Congress and consider whether or not it will even begin to solve these problems in its present form. We are all in favor of expanded funding for day care and early childhood services. The real question is—and it is probably the question over which there is the most disagreement—who should sponsor these programs. I think that the outline of needs and problems which I have just presented leads quite naturally to the kind of position the AFT has formulated.

The AFT has made an assessment of the current situation in education specifically in relation to the so-called "teacher surplus," school enrollment, and school space. The possibility of two qualified teachers existing for every job is a looming reality. We all know that classrooms are empty and schools are closing all over the country now that the baby-boom children have moved through and out of them. Between 1965 and 1973 there was a 13 percent drop in elementary and secondary school enrollment, creating seven million vacant school spaces. We think it makes sense to look at these realities in terms of new program options within the public schools. Let me run through the AFT position:

1. The AFT believes that the public school system should be the presumed prime sponsor of programs sponsored under the new bill. Where school systems are unwilling or unable to assume this responsibility others may be designated provided they meet necessary standards. We favor public control of public monies through schools and school boards as representative bodies.

2. We believe that the Federal Interagency Day Care Requirements are minimal standards which can and should be supplemented by state and local standards where these are higher.

3. We are totally against profit makers making use of these funds since their services are geared to profit margins.

4. We recognize the complexity of early learning and believe that programs should reflect varied

needs. The addition of early childhood programs to the public schools might well encourage a useful rethinking of schooling in the early
grades. We look upon the continuity between
the proposed preschool programs and existing
programs as a positive possibility. We do not
envision putting three- and four-year-olds into
the same kind of programs as now exist for older
children. I might also say here that we are mys-
tified by the view that public school prime sponsorship means rigidity and inflexibility. We see
no reason why administrative variation—in-
home care, family day care centers, etc.—
cannot occur within the public school system
providing standards are met.

5. We believe that support services such as those
discussed earlier should be provided.

6. We encourage the training and use of paraprofessionals in these programs. We recognize
the importance of extensive use of aides, and
support adult-child ratios of:
    over six years old—1 adult to 10 children
    five years old—1 adult to 7 children
    three and four years old—1 adult to 5 children
    infants—1 adult to 2 children

7. We think that with retraining and adaptation,
existing school personnel and facilities can be
used.

8. We believe that every effort should be made to
insure parent involvement in programs.

Now, I want to return to the point I made earlier about needs
and quality and how they relate to the control issue. Let me put it
simply. We do not think that a quality national program will ever come
into existence given the present arrangements. As you probably know,
day care and early childhood programs are now administered by
somewhere between 60 and 300 (unbelievably, the estimates have this
great a range) branches of the federal bureaucracy. Everyone from the
Social Security Administration to the Department of Agriculture has a
piece of the action. Then, there are all the interest groups like your
own which populate the field. I must admit that I do not understand all
the distinctions of purpose and intent that distinguish one group from

the other. But, one thing is certain—with so many competing and fragmented groups, the likelihood of mounting a unified campaign to press for and maintain comprehensive day care programs becomes all the more difficult. In other words, your effectiveness is limited.

I am reminded of the early history of the United Federation of Teachers (UFT), Local 2 of the American Federation of Teachers in New York City. Back in the 1950s before the UFT obtained collective bargaining rights to represent the city's teachers, there were many teacher groups—each with a different interest and a somewhat parochial commitment to its own turf. We had the High School Teachers Association and the elementary school group and one for the junior high level. Then too, there were the religious teachers associations and also varying political groupings. Teachers didn't have much power, but they certainly had a lot of representation. When all of these groups finally got together and realized that it would be better to organize on the basis of common interests, letting their identities as Catholics or Jews or elementary school teachers or high school teachers take a back seat to their common interests as teachers, then they finally created an organization that could do something.

Now, I do not want to carry this analogy too far. I am not suggesting that all day care interests should be in one organization. What I am suggesting is that the control, or sponsorship, question should be looked at with an eye to your effectiveness. Consider what it would mean for the potential combined clout of day care groups if all of you had some relationship to the public school system—if all of you were in some way under the public school umbrella; if your interests and the interests of other groups like you were tied up with the scope and the quality of public school sponsored programs. How much more might we be able to do in the way of day care and early childhood if your concerns about turf and the concerns of other groups like yours could be tied together in such a way that all the turf was common ground. And, in thinking about groups, you should think about the combined weight of groups that care about the public schools like the AFL-CIO, the National School Boards Association, the Chief State School Officers, the National Congress of Parents and Teachers, the American Association of School Administrators, the National Association of State Boards of Education, and even the National Education Association. These groups are all interested in public school prime sponsorship of day care. They are also the same groups who marshalled Congressional support to override a Presidential veto of a $7.9 billion education appropriations bill in the fall of 1975, which is no small feat.

If I could combine all the points I have tried to make here today I would say that the question of public school sponsorship of early childhood and day care programs is a question of quality, a question of the best use of resources, and a question of what we think we need and what is possible. Given where we are and given where I am sure most of us would agree we need to be, it seems to us at the AFT that the public school route is the best way to go.

References

Goodlad, J.I.; Klein, M.F.; and Novotney, J.M. *Early Schooling in the United States*. New York: McGraw-Hill, 1973.

Keyserling, M.D. *Windows on Day Care*. New York: National Council of Jewish Women, 1972.

U.S. Census Bureau. *School Enrollment—Social and Economic Characteristics of Students* (Advance Report). Washington, D.C.: U.S. Census Bureau, October 1974.

U.S. Department of Health, Education, and Welfare. *The Review of Child Care Service Provided Under Title IV, Social Security Act* (HEW audit). Washington, D.C.: HEW Audit Agency, November 4, 1974.

Values Examination: A Crucial Issue in Early Childhood Education

Stephanie Feeney, *Assistant Professor of Education, Department of Curriculum and Instruction, University of Hawaii, Honolulul, Hawaii.*

Carol Phelps, *Graduate Student, Department of Curriculum and Instruction, University of Hawaii, Honolulu, Hawaii.*

Doris Stanfield, *Coordinator, The Early School, Honolulu, Hawaii.*

Early childhood teacher training has traditionally been based on the view of education held by the educator responsible for conducting the training. As a result, teachers and prospective teachers of young children are often confused by inconsistencies in what they are taught in the course of their educational program. There are as many philosophies of teacher training as there are programs, and each educator gives a different perspective on what is "right" and "best" for young children and what constitutes acceptable classroom practice. Prospective teachers are rarely, if ever, given the tools and resources to examine their values and goals for children and develop their own philosophy and unique teaching style based on their beliefs.

We have concluded, based on our experience in educational settings, that educational issues cannot be discussed outside of the context of values. Teachers need the opportunity to examine their own values and develop a philosophy of teaching based on those values and beliefs. When teachers rely on the values of an outside authority they tend to jump from system to system without examining whether the various actions are consistent with one another or determining if the actions really represent their own personal values for education and children.

To clarify value questions and to aid teachers in analyzing their actions and the practices of others, we have developed a self-examination instrument called the "Dimensions of Educational Structure" (DES). The DES consists of a series of continua which illustrate some of the value choices an educator faces in designing an educational program (Fig. 1).

The value choices in the DES involve essential components of early childhood programs and lead from abstract and theoretical questions to practical program considerations. For each of the choices we present the two extreme positions. In reality, most educational decisions probably fall on the continuum somewhere between these extreme positions.

Most early childhood programs fall more to one side or the other of the continua. Program decisions with regard to each of the continua will be based on the values the teacher brings to the situation, the needs of the children, educational policies affecting the program, and the values of the parents and community.

It is important to define *values* to more fully understand its role in educational decisions. Values may be defined as goals, attitudes, feelings, and beliefs personally prized by an individual that have been chosen based on information and experience and stand the test of challenge by others with different knowledge and experience. According to this definition many key educational issues fall into the values category. In fact, much that goes on in the classroom is reflective of the teacher's values.

We have found the DES helps teachers examine their own values and bridges the gap between what they value in a global sense and how their values are actually implemented in the classroom. Teachers can indicate where their own values are located on the various dimensions and then evaluate the fit between practice and individual valuing. Teachers can also use the DES to examine the programs of others and to help share and compare educational values with parents and administrators.

If the teacher can clarify his/her values and if the teachers, parents, and administrators can become clear on the values they want to incorporate in educational programs, then they can focus on choosing the most effective programs and practices that aim toward the consensus values.

The DES reflects a major educational debate between the advocates of "learner-centered" and "content-centered" education. Major issues in this debate include whether curriculum for children should emphasize development of specific skills or development of the whole person, whether education should produce people who conform to

130

Figure I
DIMENSIONS OF EDUCATIONAL STRUCTURE

"LEARNER-CENTERED" EDUCATION	*"CONTENT-CENTERED"* EDUCATION
Values and Goals	
Development of the whole person	Development of understandings and skills
Autonomy	Conformity
Theory	
People as growth-seeking	People as shaped by the environment
Motivation to learn intrinsic	Motivation to learn extrinsic
Interactions	
Learner initiated	Teacher initiated
Relationship oriented	Task oriented
Relationships based on respect	Relationships based on authority
Curriculum Experiences	
Active learner	Receptive learner
Experiential	Abstract Symbolic
Exphasis on process	Emphasis on product
Based on needs and interests of learner	Set curriculum for all learners
Activities chosen by learner	Activities chosen by teacher
Subject areas interrelated	Subject areas separate
Organization	
Learner chosen use of time	Teacher chosen use of time
Learner chosen use of space	Teacher chosen use of space
Learner chosen use of equipment	Teacher chosen use of equipment
Evaluation	
Assessment as basis for planning	Test scores as basis for grouping
Assessment of individual growth	Grading based on norm

the demands of society as it now exists or who are creative and independent, and whether education should be based on mastery of a prescribed curriculum or based on the needs and interests of the learner.

Advocates of extreme approaches tend to be highly critical of the opposing viewpoint. Those who favor learner-centered education feel strongly that the whole child must be nurtured and that all areas of development (social, emotional, cognitive, and physical) are equally important if we are to produce adults who are humane, creative, and who can deal with the problems of a rapidly changing world. Those who favor content-centered education feel that the most important task of education is the teaching of predetermined skills and understandings which provide the basic tools for functioning in society.

We believe that neither of the extremes of these viewpoints is the optimum condition for all children, all teachers, and all parents. It is possible for both learner-centered and content-centered approaches to provide valuable educational experiences for children. A content-centered program may place heavy emphasis on academic skills and be successful in teaching these skills. A learner-centered program may emphasize other areas of development and be successful in achieving its objectives in these areas. There is no evidence to prove that any of these goals is better than the other in terms of the development of children.

If the potential worth of one program over another has its roots in what an individual values, it becomes unnecessary and impractical to argue over specific educational practices which are the reflection of a set of values. The differences of opinion that exist about educational goals can be viewed as based on value differences rather than unresolvable disputes about which educational practice is "best."

There are two principal factors which contribute to the formation of educational values: the assumptions one makes about people as learners, and the views one has about society. Educators whose life experiences have led them to believe or feel that people are basically growth-seeking and motivated by an innate desire to learn and grow will structure their classrooms in a way that allows the learner freedom to make many educational choices. Educators whose life experience leads them to see people as basically receptive and molded by the environment will structure classrooms so that the teacher makes major decisions and controls reinforcements in ways that insure that children will learn and grow in ways defined as valuable by the instructor.

Teachers who feel that the world demands people who are autonomous, active, creative, and capable of adapting to a constantly changing world will make decisions which they believe will aid children to develop in these directions. Teachers who feel that society requires that people conform to requirements of existing structures through mastering a body of existing knowledge will make educational decisions which are consistent with that view. Teachers who hold the latter view of the function of people in society act as providers of knowledge and the major source of wisdom and authority in the lives of children. Teachers who hold the former view are more likely to play a facilitative role in the lives of children in which they see their primary tasks as providing a structured environment rich in materials for learning and providing materials and interactions which challenge children to experience and inquire.

Once a teacher is clear on his/her basic values and educational goals for children, the quality of teaching is very closely related to the ability to implement these goals and values in actual classroom practice.

It is not uncommon to find that what teachers actually *do* is in direct contradiction to stated goals. For example, a teacher may value stimulating inquiry in children yet ask questions which have one predetermined answer, discouraging student questions and exploration. The teacher may not realize that an unplanned effect of the behavior is to communicate that it is not acceptable to inquire. A teacher may claim to value student autonomy, but may structure learning experiences that discourage independence. The unplanned effect of this behavior is to encourage conformity rather than autonomy. When a teacher is not careful to maintain consistency between actions and philosophies, results may be achieved which were not planned for and possibly not desired.

Children tend to do what adults *do* regardless of what they say. Consequently the behavior that the teacher models in the classroom is very important. Experiments have demonstrated that children can learn either aggressive tendencies or cooperative behaviors through teacher modeling, that children who observe adults in problem-solving tasks are able to solve problems more readily than those who have not had the observational experience, and that the level of thinking expressed in teacher statements serves to set the level for student thinking. Thus, children's behavior will be substantially influenced by the teacher's behavior in the classroom (Good and Brophy 1973, p. 116; Saiwin 1969, chap. 2).

The quality of educational experience is greatly influenced by teacher values, but these can only really impact on the lives of children in the ways intended when teacher behavior is congruent with these values.

An important component of a good early childhood program is that the teacher's values are consistent with classroom practice. It follows from this that congruence between philosophy and behavior is a more important determinant of program quality than the particular philosophic viewpoint chosen.

We strongly emphasize the area of teacher values because it has rarely been considered in teacher training. There are two other components, in addition to behavior consistent with values, which are needed to insure that programs produce maximum growth in young children.

The first of these is classroom practice which rests on a firm base of knowledge of child development. A teacher who knows how children learn and grow might place a heavy emphasis on cognitive development but would not require that children sit quietly at tables for long periods of time filling out ditto sheets. Similarly, a teacher who values the development of autonomy and who bases behavior on knowledge of child development would not allow children to run wild in a chaotic environment.

Finally, there are some basic personal qualities of teachers which have been described by Rogers (1969) and others which appear to be of great significance in determining the quality and effectiveness of early childhood programs. A good teacher of young children needs to have the characteristics that Rogers attributes to the "fully functioning person." These include the qualities of awareness and acceptance of self and the ability to respond to others in ways which are congruent with one's true feelings. The personal quality of caring for and respecting children as human beings who are valuable in their own right is another crucial attribute of teachers of young children. We will use the term "authentic" to describe teachers who manifest these qualities.

Aspects of the interaction between values and teacher qualities can be graphically portrayed. We can dichotomize value choices made in early childhood programs as primarily falling on the learner-centered or content-centered sides of the continua (Fig. 2).

We may then divide teachers into two groups based on the personal quality of authenticity (Fig. 3).

We then overlay these two figures and create a four part division which represents the interaction between value choices and teacher qualities (Fig. 4).

Quadrant I represents the kind of teacher we tend to idealize in traditional nursery school settings—the authentic, caring teacher in a learner-centered setting.

Quadrant II represents a "laissez-faire" teacher who may let

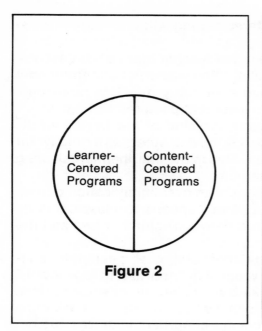

Figure 2

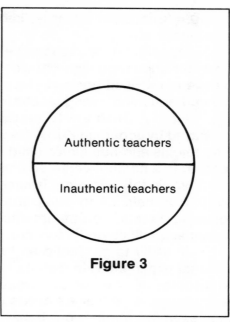

Figure 3

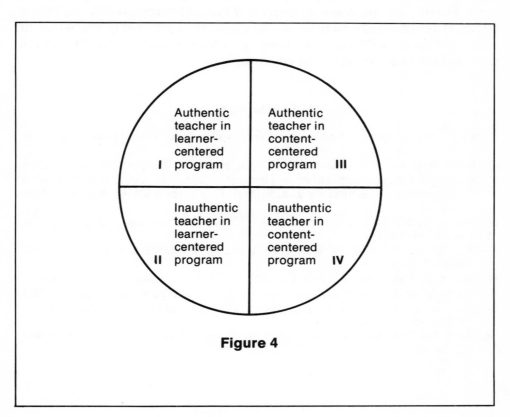

Figure 4

children function in a learner-centered setting without much nurture or support.

Quadrant III represents the kind of teacher many of us describe from our childhood with phrases like: "She was strict and traditional but we really liked her and I learned a lot that year." This represents the authentic and caring teacher in a content-centered setting.

Finally, Quadrant IV represents the kind of teacher so vividly portrayed by Jonathan Kozol, Herbert Kohl, and others as a rigid tyrant who rejects and humiliates children. This is the inauthentic, rejecting teacher in a content-centered classroom.

While this paradigm is necessarily an oversimplification of reality, it may help us to think about what happens in classrooms by focusing attention on the interaction between value choices and the personal qualities of the teacher.

In order to give children the richest and most meaningful educational experiences in their early years, it is important to look inward to discover what we value—what kind of society we desire and what kind of people we feel are needed to make that society work. We must then examine whether our behaviors are congruent with what we believe. Finally, we must ask whether our classroom practices are based on what we know about how young children learn and grow, whether we are in touch with our own feelings, and whether we communicate our respect and caring to the children.

References

Good, T., and Brophy, J. *Looking at Classrooms.* New York: Harper and Row, 1973.

Jackson, P. *Life in Classrooms.* New York: Holt, Rinehart and Winston, 1968.

Karpius, D. "Developing Teacher Competencies." In *Developing Teacher Competencies,* edited by J. Weigand. Englewood Cliffs, N.J.: Prentice-Hall, 1971.

Keliher, A. *Talks with Teachers.* Darien, Conn.: Educational Publishing Corporation, 1958.

Raths, L., and Simon, S. *Values and Teaching.* Columbus, Ohio: Charles E. Merrill, 1966.

Rogers, C.R. *Freedom to Learn.* Columbus, Ohio: Charles E. Merrill, 1969.

Rokeach, M. *Beliefs, Attitudes and Values.* San Francisco: Jossey-Bass, 1968.

Saiwin, E. *Evaluation and the Work of the Teacher.* Belmont, Calif.: Wadsworth, 1969.

Seaberg, D.I. *The Four Faces of Teaching.* Pacific Palisades, Calif.: Goodyear, 1974.

Training Pediatricians in Mental Health Aspects of Early Child Care

or
A Hospital Is No Place to Learn about Kids

Elizabeth M. Fox, *Psychologist, Child Development Unit, Children's Hospital Medical Center, Boston, Massachusetts.*

The Child Development Unit of the Children's Hospital Medical Center in Boston has initiated a program to help pediatricians learn more about the normal development of young children. In this program, we as pediatricians and psychologists collaborate with day care center teachers and administrators to provide firsthand, supervised experiences with young children for medical students and pediatricians in training. We see this program as implementing the point of view our Unit espouses that pediatricians must be child advocates and experts on "the whole child," a philosophy we hope will receive increasing emphasis in pediatric training.

Trends both in the medical world and in society are creating conditions in which pediatricians must deal not only with physical illness but with behavioral problems and all the vicissitudes of normal growth. As powerful medicines and hospital techniques have reduced the threats of disease, parents have been turning increasingly to pediatricians for help in everyday issues of parenting and childrearing ("pediatricians" refers to all health personnel working with children, such as school nurses, nurse practitioners, etc.).

It is not hard to see why parents are looking for help. Young parents often have little experience in caring for children, having often come from nuclear rather than extended families. Frequently away from their relatives and friends, isolated for long hours with small children each day, or snatching moments for child-rearing away from demanding jobs, living in a society where no one seems to have the time or interest to sit and be with or talk about small children, mothers and fathers hold out the hope for guidance and encouragement from their pediatricians. Moreover, calling the nurse or pediatrician does not have the stigma attached to contacting a psychiatrist or social worker, so that the medical caregiver is often the first professional notified in a family crisis.

Pediatricians are uniquely unsuited by their training to meet these new needs. At the end of specialty training, a pediatrician has typically *never* spent time with children outside the hospital or clinic setting. Hospital and clinic experiences preclude learning about the normal range of children's behavior or about the strengths and coping mechanisms children employ. Pediatricians at the end of training come away with a potpourri of strategies for handling particular situations (like how to calm the child before various procedures, how to talk to mothers about their children's sickness) but have little conceptual basis for the methods they employ. Pediatricians in practice, dealing with well children and their families over time, often gain a certain expertise in talking about common problems, but they share the same pragmatic, poorly conceptualized approach as the young doctors just out of training.

What the Child Development Unit tries to provide through day care experiences to doctors in training is a "gut-understanding" of some key concepts developed by child psychologists, educators, and others which form current theoretical structures upon which the science (or art) of child development is being built. These key concepts will not seem new to you, yet most doctors, although they may have heard of them, have few systematic ideas about their implications or implementation.

By elucidating these concepts within the context of day care, we provide a way of organizing and systematizing one's understanding of young children which is applicable in any pediatric encounter, be it seeing well children in the office, organizing a therapeutic regime for a chronically ill child, or facing acutely ill children in the hospital. The following list of key ideas is not exhaustive, but forms the basis of what we try to cover.

● Drawing from the work of Bowlby (1969, 1973), Ainsworth (1970), and others, attachment and separation experiences are viewed as crucial episodes in the life of a young child. Concrete illustrations of the impact of separations and attachments are often observed in the day care setting.

• Children are individuals, with inborn temperamental predispositions as well as differences based on their environments. Here we draw heavily on the insights of Lois Murphy (1962) and her colleagues in the preschool years, and to people such as Brazelton (1969), Escalona (Westman 1973), and Thomas, Chess, and Birch (Westman 1973), in the first year of life.

• Mastery and competence are driving forces in early childhood. Children can muster many coping strategies to meet new situations, challenges, defeats, and are strongly motivated to influence and understand their world. The child is a shaper, not just a receiver. We draw here on the analyses of Robert White (1960), Piaget (Ginsburg and Opper 1969), Murphy, and the recent infant literaure, such as Brazelton's (1974), on the active quality of the child.

• Age makes a difference. Although obvious, this principle is rarely applied in more than global fashion. The cognitive staging by Piaget and the affective-social staging of Freud and Erikson (1964) are seen as basic to any model of young children's development.

• Adults are important to children. This idea is central to the notion of attachment as well as to cognitive and moral development. Urie Bronfenbrenner's (1974) critique of the isolation of generations in American society is particularly relevant here.

• Adults have feelings when they work with young children, and these feelings must always be taken into consideration. This idea is basic to the therapeutic endeavor, but is necessary to good pediatric practice as well. Particular illustrations of all these principles will be referred to in the discussion of how pediatricians experience them within a day care setting.

The actual arrangements of the day care experience can be briefly summarized: Fellows (pediatricians who spend two years gaining intensive training in child development), pediatricians in training, and medical students on elective spend two or three half-days a week in a day care classroom for one to two months. They meet weekly at the Unit with staff members to discuss their experiences. We also observe them in the classrooms. They are sent as participants, not observers, and are expected to be directly involved with the children, under the teacher's supervision. They must be ready to change a diaper, tie shoes, and set the table, as well as to enjoy the more uplifting moments of being with small children.

We have regular arrangements with three centers: Brookline Children's Center, started by a local task force of NOW with a heterogeneous group of over 100 children in four programs covering the one to seven age range; Parkway Nursery and Daycare Center, started for employees at the Boston Hospital for Women, with roughly 25 three- to five-year-olds; and Hawthorne House, a large center with a working class group of children, ages two to six, funded through local and federal agencies. Our arrangements with these centers are largely informal, although one center requested that a Fellow be on their Board, and we do provide some pediatric and psychological consultative time.

What happens when doctors are sent to daycare centers? To put it most strongly, they don't like it. Even the most sympathetic and sophisticated of them are disoriented in their new role. In the hospital, pediatricians have little sustained contact with children—spending three or four hours in a group of children is unnerving. In the hospital, doctors typically see one child at a time, a child who is often motorically restricted and emotionally stressed. In day care, the doctor is outnumbered and outdistanced by assertive, vigorous children who are not intimidated by just another adult in blue jeans. Doctors in hospitals are used to giving orders. Receiving them from day care teachers is often hard to tolerate. This problem is often exacerbated by the reversal of male and female roles, the males being mostly in charge in medicine, the females more commonly in charge in day care.

Pediatricians typically return from their first day or two expressing anger at the center, feeling sorry for the children, overwhelmed by their failure to establish control, and astonished at how involved they got. Although pediatricians who are already parents are often more philosophical about their reactions, they tend to run head-on into day care staff over how to interact with the children, and often come away as upset as those who don't have children.

The pediatricians frequently project their own inner confusion onto the center—they fail to see the strong attachments among caregivers and children, nor do they perceive any structure to the day's activities. They almost invariably feel that the centers are messy and dirty (anything would be compared to the sterile environment of the hospital), and fail to see any positive virtues in the kind of "creative clutter" which characterizes most good centers. They return to the safety of the Unit weary and perplexed as to why spending a few hours with a bunch of small children should present any problems. After all, haven't they been working with kids for years?

The reason I stress this inevitable strong reaction is to emphasize the need for supervision. Just sending health professionals into day care has little value and may be counterproductive.

We know by now that doctors will have certain predictable experiences in day care which can be drawn on to help them learn. Many of these happen on the first visit, but only some can be discussed then. The others must wait until the doctors gain more understanding and assurance in the setting. I would like to mention some of these common experiences and link them to the concepts outlined earlier.

The first issue we confront is the pediatricians' own feelings about being in the setting. While many positive interactions occur with staff and children, two troublesome situations almost inevitably arise. With staff, the doctors will see situations they feel they could have handled better than the staff member. Last summer, for example, we were able to resolve a struggle between a doctor and a teacher only through a four-way conference with the teacher, the center director, myself, and the doctor. (The doctor forgot the meeting, which didn't help. . . .) These tense situations are used as illustrations of how strongly all adults feel about small children and how necessary it is for adults to work together to keep the child's best interests foremost.

The doctors are often put off by the children's indifference or refusals to be friendly. One medical student was hurt when an overture he made was greeted by "shut up." When the same student, who was well-loved by the children, announced that his last day had arrived, several children applauded. We try to use these episodes to illustrate the coping mechanisms which children may use to deal with emotional moments and to realize that the charming frankness of small children must be accepted in all its manifestations.

Another issue which we approach early is that of attachment and separation. We urge the doctors to build in from the beginning an understanding with the children that their time at the center will be over soon. They fail to see the full import of doing this until close to their departure, when they are astonished to see how sad they are feeling about leaving the center. Predictably, the doctors will forget to mention their imminent departure to children they have grown especially close to, and we discuss why they find this so difficult.

We focus on the separation of children and parents by having the pediatricians watch how leave takings are handled. Does the day care teacher spend a few moments with the parent when a child arrives? Are the teachers aware when a new child wanders into the room? What comforts do they offer a child who is distressed by separation? We also encourage them to notice the rituals which each family develops for coping with the separation and to see that many different styles can work.

A third expectable phenomenon in our discussions is the pediatricians' tendency to concentrate on the most disturbed, disturbing, or developmentally delayed children in the setting. This happens partly because day care staff are eager for any professional input they can find, but also because it provides a comfortable focus on pathology for the doctor. He or she, without even realizing it, does what comes most easily, concentrating on individual children with definable problems while remaining unable to think systematically about strengths or to be aware of the impact of the group.

Our pediatricians frequently get into trouble with staff around these difficult children, since they fail to see the maneuvers that staff have used already, and believe that they have the answer to the child's problem. Over time, they are often able to appreciate the careful, long-term planning which such children require. This is not to deny the positive impact which the pediatricians often do have in calling attention to a problem, providing new insights, or successfully working as the child's advocate with, rather than against, the center staff.

Pediatricians' concerns about individual children can lead them toward a more sophisticated appreciation of individual differences in temperament, activity level, and style of interaction. We often focus this discussion around how they have been approached by different children and how children catch their interest. One child, for example, is quiet and serious; she rarely initiates interaction. Yet her smile is so rewarding and her delight in favorite activities so complete, that she compels the attention of everyone. An abrasive style may be equally compelling—the little boy who initiated contact by saying "shut up," riveted the attention of the medical student upon him, and this student became an effective advocate for the child in a setting which has trouble tolerating his negative outbursts.

Understanding the difference age makes in the child's behavior often comes up in two situations to which the doctors react strongly. The first is the reaction of male doctors to the flirtatious behavior of three- and four-year-old girls in their classes. This behavior has a number of likely explanations in Freudian or Eriksonian theory, which the pediatricians only belatedly remember, long after they have experienced some strong feelings (positive and negative) about being overrun by little girls.

A second observation they puzzle over is why sex-role stereotyping and same-sex play increase as the children get older, only partially mitigated by nonsexist curricula, etc. Not having a well-worked out cognitive or affective developmental framework, they can't understand why, in settings where children are encouraged to play across sexes and engage in non-sex-stereotypic behavior, such patterns should persist. Clearly some of this behavior persists because of cultural attitudes, but we also discuss why children of this age tend to perceive only the most obvious trappings of the male and female role, while having a tremendous need, because of developmental stage, to define themselves as feminine or masculine.

One of the most important realizations pediatricians come to over the course of their day care experience is that adults and children have much to learn from each other. Early on, they realize how highly they are valued by the children who often crowd around, demanding affection, assistance, instruction, protection, and all the things that young children—and all of us—need. Only as they continue, however, do they realize how much the children have given to them. They begin to really understand the richness and variety of the young child, each one's sensitivities and strengths, the child's ability to touch the hearts of adults, to bring a fresh outlook and a disarming immediacy to human interactions.

Pediatricians and medical students completing their day care experience are enthusiastic about what they have learned and see important applications to their clinical work. The liveliness and vigor of children outside the hospital makes them begin to question why hospitalized children look sad and listless. Their observations of well-handled, brief separations in settings familiar to the child give them a fuller appreciation of small children's feelings when separated from their parents in the strange, painful hospital. They have a much more realistic and detailed appreciation of children's strengths and coping styles as well as a better understanding of their own skills and vulnerabilities in interacting with small children.

This training exposure has also generated research projects within the Child Development Unit. Two Fellows, Dr. Daniel Rosenn and Dr. Laurel Harken, responding to the chaos they felt upon entering a center, devised an evaluation method for pediatricians to use in day care, and validated the instrument in a number of centers. Another Fellow, Peter Paladin, worked on a project for using day care experience to improve the quality of pediatricians' well-child interviews. His preliminary results suggest that pediatricians did show increased sensitivity to the needs of children and parents as a result of their experiences in day care.

To sum up, we are excited and pleased with the active involvement and learning our doctors experience through participation in day care. We see this program as an important way of establishing a mutually beneficial dialogue between two groups of early childhood specialists and hope this model will prove useful in medical education.

References

Ainsworth, M.D.S., and Bell, S.M. "Attachment, Exploration and Separation: Illustrated by the Behavior of One-Year-Olds in a Strange Situation."*Child Development* 41 (1970): 49-67.

Bowlby, J. *Attachment and Loss, Volumes I and II.* New York: Basic Books, 1969 and 1973.

Brazelton, T. B. *Infants and Mothers: Differences in Development.* New York: Delacorte, 1969.

Brazelton, T. B. *Toddlers and Parents.* New York: Delacorte, 1974.

Bronfenbrenner, U. "The Origins of Alienation." *Scientific American,* August 1974, 53 ff.

Erikson, E. *Childhood and Society.* 2nd ed. New York: Norton, 1964.

Ginsburg, H., and Opper, S. *Piaget's Theory of Intellectual Development.* Englewood Cliffs, N.J.: Prentice-Hall, 1969.

Murphy, L. *The Widening World of Childhood.* New York: Basic Books, 1962.

Westman, J., ed. *Individual Differences in Children.* New York: Wiley, 1973.

White, R. W. "Competence and the Psychosexual Stages of Development." In *Nebraska Symposium on Motivation, 1960,* edited by M. Jones. Omaha, Nebr.: University of Nebraska Press, 1960.

The Child Development Associate Consortium's Assessment System

At the 1975 NAEYC Conference, CDA Consortium officials made several presentations in which the Consortium's recently implemented assessment system was described. The Consortium has elected to combine the content of these seminars into a single article which describes the assessment system and addresses those elements of this innovative development in the early childhood field that are most often of concern to the public.

It is fitting that the Child Development Associate Consortium had a part in the Conference, since NAEYC and the Consortium have been allied from the Consortium's beginning: NAEYC is one of the three charter members of the Consortium; Marilyn Smith, NAEYC's Executive Director, is a member of the Consortium's Board of Directors; and the new Executive Director of the Consortium is Evangeline H. Ward, a former President of NAEYC.

Evangeline H. Ward, *Executive Director, Child Development Associate Consortium, and the* **CDA Staff,** *Washington, D.C.*

What is The Child Development Associate Consortium?

The Child Development Associate Consortium was established in June 1972 to assess the competence of child care personnel and to grant credentials to those persons assessed as competent. The Consortium is a private, nonprofit corpora-

149

tion, composed of 39 national associations which have a direct interest in the field of early childhood education/child development. Serving on the Consortium's seventeen-member Board of Directors, along with representatives of the member organizations, are two individuals who represent the public-at-large.

The Consortium thus provides an opportunity for the various professions to work together to upgrade the quality of care for children in day care and child development centers. The Consortium's primary focus to date is on the quality of personnel working in these centers.

During its first three years, the efforts of the staff and membership of the CDA Consortium were devoted to research and experimentation aimed at devising a viable system for assessing and credentialing child care personnel. The result of these efforts is the Credential Award System which went into operation in May 1975. The first CDA credentials were awarded on July 24, 1975, to 34 persons from across the country.

During the next few years, while it continues to assess candidates and award credentials, the Consortium will also be engaged in two other important activities:

a. a continual evaluation and refinement of the Credential Award System;

b. an effort to gain wide recognition of the CDA credential, by other educators and state officials, as a standard of competence in the child care field.

What is a Child Development Associate, a CDA?

A Child Development Associate or CDA is a person able to meet the specific needs of a group of children in a child development setting by nurturing the children's physical, social, emotional, and intellectual growth; by establishing and maintaining a proper child care environment; and by promoting good relations between parents and the child development center.

While CDAs work in many different settings—Head Start programs, nursery schools, kindergartens, day care centers, church-sponsored programs, etc.—they all take primary responsibility for a given group of children. Where a special need arises, they may need to consult with a master teacher, other peer professionals, or a specialist of some kind, as is appropriate in any quality program for young children.

CDAs must possess the six kinds of competence considered by experts in the field of early childhood education/child development to be essential for a person responsible for young children in a group setting (Fig. 1, p.158).

How does an individual become a CDA?

To become a CDA, a person must demonstrate competence. First, the individual must apply to the Consortium and be accepted as a candidate for the CDA credential. All candidates are evaluated in the Consortium's assessment system. Those judged to be competent receive the CDA credential and thereby become Child Development Associates.

What are the basic features of the Consortium's assessment system?

The CDA process differs from assessment systems used by most credentialing agencies. Four distinctive elements characterize the Consortium's process.

1. *It is a team assessment.* The performance of every candidate for the CDA credential is assessed by a Local Assessment Team (LAT) composed of four persons: the CDA candidate, a trainer, a parent-community representative, and a Consortium representative. Each brings a different perspective to the team. All the members of the team, except the Consortium representative, are chosen from the candidate's community.

2. *It is a performance-based assessment.* In order to gain the CDA credential, the candidate must demonstrate competence in the six general competency areas. The candidate must compile a portfolio of materials used in working with his or her group of children. The other three mem-

bers of the team use assessment instruments provided by the consortium to observe, interview, and gather data about the candidate.

3. *It is a judgment-referenced assessment.* The Consortium relies on the coordinated human judgment of the assessment team to determine whether or not to award the candidate a CDA credential. When they have collected all their data, the members of the Local Assessment Team meet to discuss the candidate's performance. All the data collected by each member is studied by the entire team and the candidate's performance is compared with the Consortium Competency Standards, interpreted by the team in the light of the candidate's community and center situation. The team's judgments about the candidate's competence must be supported by documented evidence that can be reviewed by the Consortium.

4. *It is a verified assessment.* Every Local Assessment Team must adhere strictly to Consortium regulations in collecting data about the candidate and in conducting the team meeting. Along with the final judgment of the team (either that the candidate "should be awarded the CDA credential" or that the candidate "needs more training"), the Consortium representative must send to the Consortium all documents, including one testifying that the assessment team observed all procedural requirements in its conduct of the assessment.

Why did the Consortium choose to assess performance?

The Consortium believes that performance-based assessment is a relevant, workable method for judging competence in the child care field. In developing its system, the Consortium consulted a wide spectrum of persons interested in child care and development. Among them were practitioners, scholars, philosophers, researchers, trainers, specialists, and parents. The overriding note sounded by all was the need for a system that could judge on-site performance. There was a shared belief that a person's ability to complete a certain number of courses or to pass a written examination was not necessarily a determinant of ability to serve children in child caring programs in competent ways.

Therefore, the Consortium's assessment system puts less stress on the number of years spent or courses taken in formal education. It presumes, rather, that day-to-day value to children will show in performance with them; knowledge will also be reflected in performance, as built into the system.

The Consortium believes that performance-based assessment is also more flexible and inclusive than traditional systems, as it is designed to accommodate to ethnic and cultural diversity. It is accessible to many able individuals who, because they may have lacked an opportunity for formal education, have had no opportunity to give evidence of their competent performance with children.

As one of the first CDAs expressed it, "I think so many people have a natural knack for teaching children. If they had access to this program, think of how much good they could do. With a little help, a little understanding, a little positive teaching, there are a lot of people who could help children."

Why is the assessment made by a team?

The Consortium believes a collaborative team approach to assessment is desirable, because:

- A team of observers will collect a greater amount of relevant information on a candidate's performance than would a single observer.

- A team trying to reach a decision based on consensus will make a more valid decision than several individual decisions.

- A team composed of specialists in early childhood education/child development and representatives of the local community (including the candidate) will bring several perspectives to the assessment, which will contribute to a more sound credentialing decision.

The Consortium's concept of team assessment involves a totally collective enterprise—shared planning, implementation, review, and judgment. Having a variety of perspectives provides a means of checking perceptions, thus reducing arbitrariness in decisions or interpretations. A candidate's fate is not in any one person's hands. Further, several perspectives lend themselves to decisions based on a broader base of information.

Who are the members of the assessment team?

The four members of the Local Assessment Team are the *candidate*, whom the team observes and who supplements the team's observations with explanations and detailed information about the individual children in the group; the *trainer,* who has participated in the candidate's professional development, is well versed in the practices of early childhood education/child development, and has knowledge of and experience with child care programs in the general area served by the candidate; the *parent-community representative,* who lives in the community served by the candidate and has specific experience in the center where the candidate is assessed, also brings knowledge of the community and its cultural styles; and the *Consortium representative,* who has had direct experience in center-based programs for three- to five-year-olds, has an academic background in early childhood education/child development, and is trained in the assessment procedures and requirements established by the Consortium, and who safeguards the interests of the Consortium and its member associations in each assessement.

Each individual on the assessment team studies the candidate's performance from a unique perspective. While each LAT member collects information individually, all evaluation of the candidate's performance is done collaboratively by the entire LAT during its decision meeting.

The Consortium believes that a candidate's professional information and ability to function with children in a center in a given community will be of high importance to a team that includes both professional and community members.

**Does the Consortium provide special training
for members of assessment teams?**

The Consortium provides special training for Consortium representatives, who are responsible for the overall conduct of the assessment meetings and for ensuring that teams perform all their tasks in accordance with Consortium regulations. In order to become a Consortium representative, an individual must satisfy selection criteria and complete a five-day training program aimed at developing skill in observation and interview techniques, in promoting effective interpersonal relations, and in small-group processes. Persons who successfully complete this training program are endorsed as official representatives of the Consortium and are eligible for assignment to Local Assessment Teams.

The other three members of the Local Assessment Team receive no special training, but the Consortium has prepared special materials, including the Local Assessment Team Guidelines, which give clear and explicit directions to help them carry out their assessment duties.

Why is the candidate a member of the assessment team?

The Consortium's assessment system includes the candidate on the Local Assessment Team, for these reasons:

- The candidate is a valid source of information for use in assessment. Certain information is available only from the candidate's perspective.
- The candidate is able to clarify information on his or her performance, thereby adding to the assessment team's evidence for a valid decision.
- The candidate is better able to identify strengths and weaknesses and to receive recommendations for continued professional development.

The candidate has major responsibility for preparing for a CDA assessment. The candidate alone determines what data will become part of his or her portfolio, selects the local team members, and makes sure that all forms are prepared in readiness for the assignment of the Consortium representative.

The Consortium believes that by having the candidate take responsibility for these important matters, evidence of individual strength becomes apparent. It is vital that a climate for collaborative assessment should begin with the person who wishes to be assessed. The candidate, then, is a peer in every sense of the word, a participant from initiation to the final decision of the Local Assessment Team. It is one of the unique features of the Consortium's assessment system and distinguishes it from more traditional systems. These conditions cause the assessment to be more sensitive to the candidate's unique experiences, learning style, communication style, and general responsiveness, all of which assure a supportive, trusting, open environment in which the candidate can perform with confidence.

How does the assessment team operate?

Each team member collects information on the candidate's performance and puts it into a format designed by the Consortium to facilitate team review. The candidate compiles a portfolio and selects the trainer and parent-community representative for the Local Assessment Team. The portfolio is the candidate's major component of data and is designed to be one primary focus of discussion at the Local Assessment Team meeting.

The parent-community representative's role on the team is to report on the candidate's performance from the perspective of the community and the parents of children in the candidate's group. First, the parent-community representative surveys the parents of the children in the candidate's room using an interview-questionnaire supplied by the Consortium. Second, the parent-community representative observes the candidate working with the children and records these observations. The parent-community representative comes to the team meeting armed with a summary of the parent survey and the observation record.

The trainer is a person responsible for the pre- or in-service education of the candidate. The trainer brings a two-fold perspective to the team's deliberations. First, the trainer has known and worked with the candidate over a period of time, often on a day-to-day basis, and is thereby able to observe and report changes in the candidate's performance over time. Second, the trainer is familiar with the regulations governing child care programs in the locality. The trainer must write a summary report describing the candidate's performance in each area of functioning, and the report is entered into the team meeting.

The Consortium representative conducts a three-hour observa-

tion of the candidate and then interviews the candidate. The representative records these for entry into the team deliberations.

When all the above is complete, the assessment team holds a
formal meeting to review the documented data and to decide whether
the candidate should be recommended for a CDA credential. The
meeting is conducted in accordance with the following Consortium
guidelines:

a. All team members have an equal voice during
   the discussion, and the opinion of each has an
   equal weight in the making of the final decision;

b. Each team member must review all the data presented during the meeting;

c. The team must document its decisions;

d. Three members of the team must vote the candidate competent in order to recommend the
   candidate eligible to be awarded the CDA credential;

e. The Consortium representative must certify that
   all the procedures required by the Consortium
   were followed by the assessment team.

By what standards are candidates for the CDA credential assessed?

The core of the Consortium's assessment is the document
called Competency Standards (Fig. 1, p. 158). Within the scope of this
document are the six *general* kinds of competence that experts agree
a person must possess in order to work effectively with young children. These six competency areas have been further delineated into
functional areas. Using these, the Local Assessment Team members
collect information and assess the candidate.

For Local Assessment Team members, the Competency Standards have two basic uses:

- *Observation:* The Competency Standards serve
  to organize each Local Assessment Team
  member's observations. Each member of the
  team must collect information on the candidate's
  performance in each of the 13 functional areas.

157

Competency Structure Chart

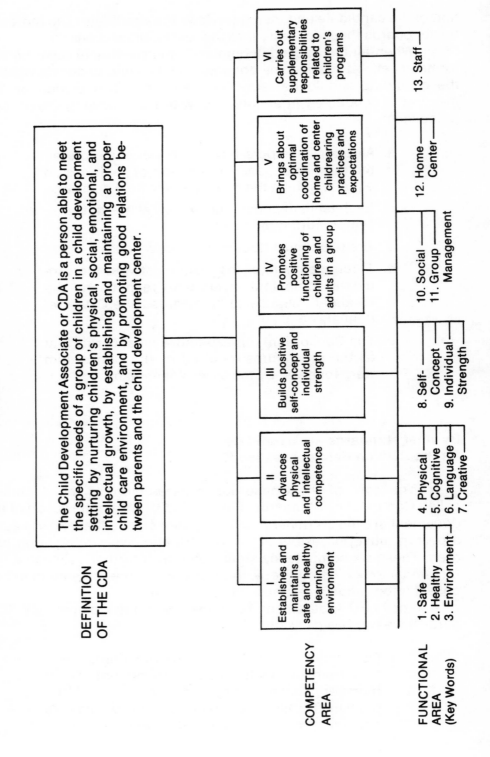

DEFINITION OF THE CDA

The Child Development Associate or CDA is a person able to meet the specific needs of a group of children in a child development setting by nurturing children's physical, social, emotional, and intellectual growth, by establishing and maintaining a proper child care environment, and by promoting good relations between parents and the child development center.

COMPETENCY AREA

I — Establishes and maintains a safe and healthy learning environment

II — Advances physical and intellectual competence

III — Builds positive self-concept and individual strength

IV — Promotes positive functioning of children and adults in a group

V — Brings about optimal coordination of home and center childrearing practices and expectations

VI — Carries out supplementary responsibilities related to children's programs

FUNCTIONAL AREA (Key Words)

1. Safe
2. Healthy
3. Environment
4. Physical
5. Cognitive
6. Language
7. Creative
8. Self-Concept
9. Individual Strength
10. Social
11. Group Management
12. Home Center
13. Staff

Figure 1

- *Judgment:* The Competency Standards are used by the team in reaching its decision about the candidate's competence. The team members study the candidate's performance and evaluate it, both specifically—as it compares to the standard in each of the 13 functional areas, and generally—as it compares to the definition of a CDA.

How does the assessment process meet the needs of the local situation?

The Consortium's Competency Standards are national in scope. As such, they are broad and flexible enough to allow for local adaptation; the mechanism for this adaptation is the Local Assessment Team. The Local Assessment Team interprets the broad Competency Standards with the help of what are called indicators. Indicators are a further refinement of the functional areas and are examples of the kind of behavior which indicate that a child care worker is performing competently. They make possible specific analyses of a candidate's performance within a local setting and may differ from situation to situation. For instance, in settings with bilingual and/or bicultural children, with handicapped children, or where a particular program philosophy is followed, etc., indicators will vary. The development of indicators is an ongoing task for the Consortium during this first year of implementing its assessment system.

Is the assessment system adaptable to different styles of curricula in early childhood programs?

The Consortium assesses individuals, not programs. However, it is a flexible system for assessing child care personnel in all types of child care settings, private and public. The particular philosophy of the program in which the candidate is working is noted by the assessment team. Then, the candidate is judged on his or her ability to perform competently within the context of that program.

Who can apply for the CDA credential?

In order to be accepted as an applicant for a CDA credential, an individual must satisfy the following requirements:

1. *Age:* The applicant must be a least sixteen years old.

2. *Access to Center:* The applicant must provide proof of access to an approved child development center, where observation by an assessment team is possible.

3. *Training:* The applicant must provide evidence of formal or informal training in early childhood education/child development: an official transcript from an accredited institution or testimony that one has attended workshops, seminars, or in-service programs.

4. *Experience:* The applicant must have had at least eight consecutive months of full-time experience working with children from three to five years old in a group setting. The applicant must have been personally responsible for the group's activities and must have worked with parents of children in the group and must be able to show evidence of that activity. If the applicant's work has been part-time, sixteen months of experience are required.

If persons are interested in becoming candidates for the CDA credential, how should they prepare themselves before applying?

Before they apply to become candidates, individuals should study the competencies and the functional areas (Fig. 1, p. 158) to gain understanding of the kind of performance expected of a would-be CDA. In the early stages of the assessment process, every candidate must compile a portfolio of materials that gives evidence of mastery of each of the CDA competencies and begin to locate local persons who are qualified and willing to serve on the assessment team. Later, while being observed by other members of the assessment team, candidates must demonstrate the CDA competencies in their work with young children. Even before entrance into the Consortium's assessment program, an individual could begin to compile a portfolio, which is a personal record of competent performance.

When an individual is ready to apply, how should she or he proceed?

First, the individual must fill out an Enrollment Form and mail it to the Consortium. The answers to the questions on the form are the basis for determining whether the individual meets the eligibility requirements listed above.

If the individual is eligible, the Consortium sends him or her an application packet, which includes an application form, a copy of the Local Assessment Team Guidelines, and materials for the candidate's trainer, parent-community representative, and center director. A $5 application fee must accompany the application form.

The individual is then registered as a candidate for assessment. The Consortium mails the necessary materials. If an application is not accepted, the applicant will be notified.

In addition to the $5 application fee, a charge of $15 will be made when a Consortium representative is assigned. Both fees are nonrefundable.

What is the value of the CDA credential? Why would people apply for it?

At present, people want the credential for professional pride and to indicate to themselves and others that they have been judged competent. When the credential is better known and established, it is likely that the CDA credential will also be valued by employers of personnel in both public and private centers. Most child care centers want people on their staffs who are known to be competent to work with young children. The CDA has a credential that testifies to the fact that he or she has demonstrated the ability to perform competently.

The assessment process is an asset to the professional development of the individual. The assessment is not a pass-or-fail process. Team members look at the candidate's performance in detail and, at the end of the assessment, present him or her with a composite portrait of strengths, weaknesses, and suggestions for improvement. The whole procedure is calculated not just to evaluate how the candidate is now performing, but to enable the candidate to perform more competently in the future. The system enables each team member to focus, throughout the process, on the functional areas where competence is considered essential to quality programming for young children.

Is the CDA credential a license?

No. Only states have the authority to issue licenses. Neither is it a replacement for state certification. Rather, it is a professional award such as lawyers and architects receive from their national professional associations.

However, five states have already recognized the CDA credential by including it in their day care licensing regulations as an option for meeting staff qualifications. The five are Kansas, Minnesota, North Carolina, North Dakota, and Washington. The Consortium has worked with other states, as well. Several states that are writing or revising their licensing standards have requested and received help from the Consortium in developing center-based staff qualifications.

Who serves on the Consortium's Board of Directors?

There are, at present, 39 national professional associations from which the Consortium's Board of Directors is elected and two individuals who are public representatives.

The officers of the Board are: Annie L. Butler, Chairperson; Maurine McKinley, Vice Chairperson; and James Becker, Secretary-Treasurer. Annie L. Butler is Professor of Education, Indiana University, Bloomington, Indiana; and a representative to the Consortium for the Association for Childhood Education International. Maurine McKinley is Associate Director of and a representative to the Consortium for the Black Child Development Institute, Washington, D.C. James Becker is Executive Director of and a representative to the Consortium for the National Foundation for the Improvement of Education, Washington, D.C.

Other Board members are: Mary Jane Anderson, American Library Association/Children's Services Division; Cecilia Blackstock,

American Association of Elementary/Kindergarten/Nursery Educators; Walter J. Cegelka, National Association for Retarded Citizens; Lucille A. Echohawk, National Indian Education Association; Margie R. Hanson, American Alliance for Health, Physical Education, and Recreation; Asa Hilliard,* Dean, School of Education, San Francisco State University; Lilian Katz,* Professor, Early Childhood Education, University of Illinois.

Also: Carol R. Lubin, National Federation of Settlements and Neighborhood Centers; Orrin Nearhoof, National Association of State Directors of Teacher Education and Certification; Greg Ochoa, National Education Task Force de la Raza; Nicomedes Sanchez, Puerto Rican Association for Community Affairs, Inc.; Bernadene Schunk, Association of Teacher Educators; and Marilyn Smith, National Association for the Education of Young Children.

How is the Consortium funded?

Up to now, the Consortium has received all its funding from the Office of Child Development (OCD), a division of the U.S. Department of Health, Education, and Welfare. However, the Consortium is not a federal agency; it is a private, nonprofit corporation. Its policy decisions are established by the Consortium membership, through its Board and staff. The Consortium is now actively seeking additional sources of funds, so that it might expand its assessment efforts.

Is the Consortium involved in training?

No, the Consortium does not conduct CDA training programs. Its training effort is geared only to preparing endorsed Consortium representatives whose roles are devoted exclusively to assessing and credentialing child care personnel.

Who does train CDAs?

CDAs receive training in early childhood education/child devel-

---

*Individual Public Representative

opment in a variety of ways, under a variety of sponsorships. Within the ranks of CDAs there is a wide range of differing amounts of education (formal and informal) and work experience. The Consortium accepts candidates in centers from all these varieties of programs since its focus is on the assessment of the competent performance of the individuals who work with three- to five-year-old children in center-based programs under both private and public sponsorship.

◇ ◇ ◇

For Enrollment Forms and for more information about the CDA Consortium's program, contact:

Evangeline H. Ward
Executive Director
The Child Development Associate Consortium
7315 Wisconsin Avenue, Suite 601E
Washington, D.C. 20014

Early Childhood Education— It's a Science!

Daniel C. Jordan, *Director, Center for the Study of Human Potential, School of Education, University of Massachusetts, Amherst, Massachusetts.*

For the past fifteen years, my colleagues and I have been laboring to establish the scientific foundations for a new comprehensive educational system called *Anisa*.* As part of this effort, we studied the history and philosophy of science so that we would have the clearest possible picture of the task we were undertaking. We not only faced the question "Is early childhood education a science?" but "Can it ever become one?" The purpose of my presentation is to explore the meaning of these questions and to propose a framework within which we can arrive at some reasonable answers to them.

What do we mean when we claim that something is a science? What do we mean when we say that something is an art? Aristotle believed there were three kinds of thought: knowing (*theoria*), doing (*praxis*), and making (*poesis*). When we discuss the doing or making of something, we are talking about the skilled application of knowledge or technique, and we usually use the word *art* to refer to such application. Since the teachers of young children have to do and make many things that require the

---

*For an overview of the Anisa Model, see Daniel C. Jordan and Donald T. Streets, "The Anisa Model: A New Basis for Educational Planning." *Young Children 28, no. 5 (June): 289-307.*

167

skilled application of knowledge, we can say that early childhood education is an art.

Knowing, on the other hand, is a kind of mental activity more associated with the idea of science—a word which comes from the Latin *scio*, which means "to know." Since what teachers of young children have to do in meeting their professional responsibilities requires knowledge, we can also say that early childhood education is a science of sorts. Our thesis, however, is that for the sake of children and the future of the nation it needs to become much more of a science, and as soon as possible.

Let us proceed, then, to gain a fuller understanding of what is meant by the term "science." It means more than knowledge; it refers to *organized* knowledge, or organized bodies of knowledge. When knowledge is organized into a body, we usually give it a name such as sociology, psychology, biology, or anthropology. Any kind of organization, however, won't make it qualify as a science. Knowledge, for instance, can be largely descriptive, i.e., statements of what happened—just a record of observations organized chronologically. You can, and do, for instance, have knowledge of what happens at your preschool on any given day and you can write up a description and share this bit of knowledge organized chronologically with someone else. Although observations are certainly crucial to the development of any science, they are not in themselves the sort of knowledge that constitutes a science, because they lack the kind of organization that yields explanations of the how and the why of the phenomena under consideration. The essence of science, then, is not knowledge merely organized in any old way, but knowledge organized to explain things, thereby fostering an understanding of them.

At the present time, knowledge pertinent to early childhood education is fragmented, noncomprehensive, conflicting, and reflects no distinction between the trivial and the most important; it is largely descriptive and therefore lacks explanatory power; and, finally, there is such a vast amount of it that it is overwhelming—simply not manageable. Clearly, a great deal of work remains to be done before we can say early childhood education is a science, or is based on a science.

One might well ask, "Is it worth all the time, effort, and expense required to make it into a science?" Our contention is that we have no other choice—early childhood education must become more of a science because we have to have explanations of the "hows" and the "whys" if we are to improve systematically what we need to do for young children. Because of the deteriorating conditions of American society in general, it looks as though we may go through a period when there will be very little support from home and community to help young children grow and develop into wholesome, stable, productive, reasonably happy, socially mature adults. Not only must we find a way of helping them to grow into stable adults, but we must help them gain a sense of moral responsibility such that they will have the inclination, inspiration, and stamina to do something about the pressing issues and problems confronting human society at this juncture in history. In my opinion, it is hardly possible to overstate the urgency in this matter.

Let me give you a quick picture of American society as reflected in startling statistics pertinent to three major pathological trends in our society: crime and delinquency, mental illness, and immorality. Unless the schools take a stronger and more definitive role in the moral education of children, children will grow up in accordance with the pathological conditions of American society. Inevitably, they will perpetuate its deterioration and be utterly impotent to reverse the trends.

In the United States a serious crime is committed every 3 seconds around the clock; a violent crime (murder, robbery, assault to kill, or forcible rape) is committed once every 33 seconds; someone is murdered every 26 minutes; every 10 minutes there is a forcible rape; once every 70 seconds there is an aggravated assault; once every 71 seconds someone is robbed and once every 10 seconds there is a burglary; larceny or theft takes place every 6 seconds; an automobile is stolen every 32 seconds. Public expenditures for the criminal justice system are over $12 billion annually. In 1972, there were 1,624,000 persons committed to hospitals because of mental illness. Double that number for those who are seeing psychiatrists or psychologists for very serious mental problems. Personal health care expenditures amounted to $80 billion in 1973. We consumed over a million and a half pounds of tranquilizers in 1972. In the same year, Americans consumed $20.3 billion worth of alcohol. To celebrate the birth of Christ last year, over 50 million gallons of distilled spirits were bought. In 1973, 11 million accidental injuries, 40 percent of the admissions to mental hospitals, and 50 percent of the arrests were attributed to alcohol. The suicide rate for alcoholics is 58 times greater than the rate for nonalcoholics. Every 18 months, drunken drivers kill as many citizens as United States soldiers killed in the whole of the Vietnam War. Each year, there is over an $8 billion economic loss directly attributable to the effects of alcohol. In 1973, there were 3,098,000 school dropouts. Out of the 60 million students enrolled in the United States, over 16 million of them are functionally illiterate. The divorce rate is increasing (soon to be one in two marriages), and child abuse and neglect are increasing as well. In a recent study of child abuse cases handled by 71 hospitals, attending physicians reported a total of 302 cases in which 33 of the children died and 85 of them sustained permanent brain damage. In a study of 447 cases handled by district attorneys, 45 of the children died and 29 sustained permanent brain damage.

Futurist Herman Kahn predicted trends in American society as a part of a study to determine what social conditions would be like in the year 2000. In the 1960s, he described a trend that was current then which he called the Increasingly Sensate Trend. This trend was characterized as:

> Worldly, naturalistic, realistic, visual, illusionistic, every-day, amusing, interesting, erotic, satirical, novel, eclectic, syncretic, fashionable, technically superb, impressionistic, materialistic, commercial and professional. (Kahn and Wiener 1967, p. 707)

He then went on to predict that by the 1970s we could expect to be in the Late Sensate Trend which he described as:

> Under-worldly, expressing protest or revolt, overripe, sensation seeking, titillating, depraved, faddish, violently novel, exhibitionistic, debased, vulgar, ugly, debunking, nihilistic, pornographic, sarcastic or sadistic. (Kahn and Wiener 1967, p. 707)

Given the distressing trends revealed by these statistics and descriptions, you can see that we need to apply every bit of knowledge we have about human growth and development to reverse some of these trends and rescue our children from what could turn into a nightmare of alarming dimensions. However, such knowledge has to become better organized before we can apply it effectively. To organize requires organizing principles—ideas of such generality that all specifics can be related to them. Such ideas may be taken as first principles. Formulating them requires philosophical or speculative thought. Up to the present time, early childhood education has been practically devoid of this kind of thinking.

The First Principles of the Anisa Theory

What would you say are the first principles of your profession—the first principles of early childhood education? We have asked thousands of teachers that question and have never received a clear response. Professors who teach in schools of education have, of course, rarely thought of first principles in practical terms; otherwise, they no doubt would have discussed them and made their students aware of them. Without first principles, our knowledge about early childhood education cannot be usefully organized, and to that extent it cannot be very scientific. The great biologist Julian Huxley wrote:

> The lack of a common frame of reference, the absence
> of any unifying set of concepts and principles, is now, if
> not the world's major disease at least its most serious
> symptom. (1960, p. 88)

Our work in formulating the Anisa Model entailed a ten-year struggle to identify and clarify the first principles of early childhood education so we could develop it into a science.

From first principles it is possible to deduce a coherent body of theory which can then function as an effective and efficient guide to practice. Efficiency simply means being able to accomplish what you want to accomplish in a reasonable time without a wasteful or needless expenditure of resources. According to Alfred North Whitehead, the mathematician and logician on whose philosophy we have drawn heavily in formulating the Anisa Model, incoherence comes from disconnectedness, arbitrariness, or incompatibility among first principles (Whitehead 1960). We therefore took special care to make certain that all of the first principles we were formulating were free from conflicts and that they were all logically interrelated.

Since people are the subject and object of education, it only makes good sense that we should first settle our minds on a view of human nature before trying to design an education system. Our first principles therefore set forth propositions about human nature. Because so many educational innovations in the last ten years have evaporated without leaving a trace, we wanted to make certain that Anisa rested on the most solid foundation—that its first principles would have already in some sense stood the test of time. To arrive at the philosophical basis of the Model, we reviewed 2300 years of thinking about human nature. We started with Parmenides, perhaps the most important philosopher before Plato, and examined both Eastern and Western streams of philosophical thought right up to the present time. The Anisa Model therefore does not just rest on the feeble views of a few university scholars but on a careful synthesis of the best thinking about humanity and destiny that history has ever recorded.

In the course of the struggle to develop the philosophical foundations of the Model, it became clear to us that understanding human nature is impossible apart from considering how people see themselves related to the universe. People are conscious beings, and one of the by-products of consciousness is a recognition that people are distinct and separate from all other things in creation. That recognition sustains the intuition that each person can also have a relationship to all of those other things. Thus, a fundamental characteristic of the individual is an inner pressure to know how one is related to everything in the cosmos, including the ultimate unknowns or unknowables. This eternal quest for knowing and wanting to belong reflects two basic human characteristics—knowing and loving; the interplay between these two capacities makes each person capable of infinite evolutionary development.

Thus, our first principle concerning human nature is that each is endowed with infinite potentiality—that we have no rational justification for conceptualizing limits to the expression of people's potentialities. Each person is, then, an open system, capable of perpetual refinement and development. We accepted Whitehead's proposition that reality inheres in the process of translating potentiality into actuality—a process he equates with creativity. Unlimited creativity and continual becoming are therefore human realities. This proposition became the justification for establishing an educational model based on the idea of process. From the point of view of the Anisa Model, it is the purpose of education to facilitate the translation of the child's potentialities into actuality at an optimum rate, and it is a function of theory and research to find out what blocks or inhibits the actualization of potentiality so that we can avoid its suppression on the one hand and facilitate its actualization on the other.

The Anisa theory of development explains what human potentialities are and how they are actualized. The Anisa theories of curriculum and pedagogy are derived from the theory of development. Thus, what is taught and how it is taught is compatible with the essential nature of human development. In brief, the Anisa theory of development identifies two categories of potentialities: biological and psychological. The theory fixes nutrition as the key factor in the actualization of biological potentialities and establishes learning as the key factor in the actualization of psychological potentialities. Psychological potentialities are divided into five categories: psychomotor, perceptual, cognitive, affective, and volitional. The process curriculum is designed to actualize potentialities in these five categories at an optimum rate. The theory of development establishes interaction with the environment as the means by which learning takes place and the psychological potentialities of the child are actualized. From this proposition we have a definition of teaching: arranging environments and guiding the child's interaction with them to actualize particular potentialities. Good teaching presupposes being able to diagnose the developmental level of the child so that appropriate environments can be arranged and the child's interaction with them be facilitated so that potentialities are actualized. This definition of teaching enables us to break down the teaching act into its smallest elements and thereby give aspiring teachers the most detailed and constructive feedback on their efforts to become good teachers. We have in the Anisa Model the conceptual basis of a truly competency-based teacher preparation program.

The total body of Anisa theory also includes a theory of administration and a theory of evaluation. We found that administrators of educational systems can very easily make decisions which undermine the very purpose of their institution. It is therefore important for them to understand the first principles of the profession; otherwise, they will make decisions which lead to a distribution of resources not in keeping with purpose and priorities. Our theory of evaluation is an indispensable aid to good administration. It focuses attention on what kinds of data should be collected and how they should be analyzed in order to yield information that will be useful to the improvement of practice through the refinement of theory and the accumulation of empirical knowledge.

The basic assertions about human nature and the main propositions of the theories of development, curriculum, teaching, administration, and evaluation are the first principles of this new comprehensive educational system designed for the year 2000 and beyond. We have used them to organize the vast amount of information presently available about human growth, development, and learning. Over 740 periodicals pertinent to human development are published monthly. The libraries are filled with information. Without first principles there is no effective way to organize it and until it is organized it can't be digested, understood, and used.

The Value of Theory

Because educators are sometimes hostile toward theory, I feel impelled to make a few comments about it. Many people in the profession feel that the word *theory* simply refers to a realm of thought that has nothing to do with the practical. Students in education often use the phrase "too theoretical" as a damning criticism of courses. In fact, theory is the best friend a practitioner ever had; "there is nothing so practical as a good theory." As theories are applied, experience is illumined, understanding is strengthened, and our effectiveness increased. With increased scientific knowledge we are able to predict what will happen if we do certain things. Predictability leads to accountability. (Incidentally, requiring accountability before the means of predictability are in hand is an unworkable proposition. For this reason the movement for accountability in education is premature; we have to have a science first.)

Theories bring order to thought about means-ends relationships. As theories are applied, we begin to see patterns among natural phenomena. When these patterns are consistently present under particular circumstances, we call them laws. Thus, when ordered thought is focussed on repeated changes in the human life cycle, laws of development can be discerned. Laws contain only terms that refer to observables. Theories, on the other hand, contain at least some terms that do not refer to observables (such as electrons, electromagnetic waves, neutrons, curvature of space, etc.). Laws explain the facts; theories explain laws. Since theories speak to unobservables, such as the learning that goes on inside the child's brain, we have to have some way of making a connection between theoretical language and the experimental or practical language. This is a big problem in the field of early childhood education. It is the purpose or function of a model to make the connection between the theoretical and the practical. The Anisa Model represents a massive translation of an extensive body of theory into practical terms. We now have twenty years of research on the drawing boards. I think we have clearly articulated every major question that needs to be answered to advance early childhood education and, in many cases, we have expressed them in the form of testable hypotheses which will guide many of our research efforts in the years to come. The essential point here is that systematic progress is not possible without science and science is not possible without theory.

The work of B.F. Skinner, for example, suffers from an antitheory bias that leads to self-contradictions which undermine the logic of the system and therefore weaken it. He has tried to base his "science" only on descriptions of things observed; he therefore dismisses the importance of what goes on inside the head, which is not observable. In other words, he is interested in only stimulus inputs and behavioral outputs, both of which are observable. Unfortunately, this interest in laws and denial of the usefulness of theory leads to difficulties. While certain laws of behavior which he has articulated explain many of the facts, the laws themselves need explanation and that requires theory. In the absence of theories to explain laws, the laws will be made to do more work than they are capable of doing. For example, if you put a rat in a Skinner box, it will sniff around and eventually press a lever which will release a food pellet into the box. The lever is the stimulus, pressing it is the response, and the food pellet is the reinforcement. A reinforcement following a response to a stimulus increases the probability that the same response will be given in the presence of the same stimulus on a subsequent occasion. This explanation is useful as far as it goes, but it does not really account for how the rat learned to press the lever. It already had to know how to press the lever before it could get the reinforcer—the food pellet. In the Skinnerian system, then, you already have to know how to do something before it can be reinforced. What is learned is not that "something," but that you can get a reward for doing what you already know how to do. Although Skinner denies the importance of what goes on inside the head, both the terms *stimulus* and *reinforcer* take their definitions from internal states. A stimulus is any external event which can elicit a response from the organism. If the organism doesn't respond, then you can't call it a stimulus. Therefore the stimulus takes its definition from an internal state of the organism. The same is true for a reinforcement. A reinforcement is anything that increases the probability of a certain response following a given stimulus. If you give the organism something and it doesn't increase the probability of the response that it follows, then you can't call it a reinforcement. For example, a child who has a painful allergy to chocolate candy would not feel "reinforced" by receiving such candy immediately after a given response. The allergic reaction is determined by particular internal states of the organism. Or, to take a more obvious example, the child's memories influence what will be regarded as stimuli and what will be regarded as reinforcers. It is hard to consider memory as something other than an internal state of the organism. A two-month-old child cannot respond to the stimulus "2 + 2," nor can we get a response of the answer "4" so that it could be reinforced. The child can't respond to the stimulus "2 + 2" because he does not have certain internal structures that enable him to make sense out of "2 + 2" as a stimulus. He can't even say the word "four" because certain linguistic structures in the speech and motor areas of the brain have not yet been developed.

The purpose of this Skinnerian digression is not to deny the usefulness of what Skinner has discovered but simply to show its limitations. His denial of the usefulness of theory is part and parcel of his denial of the usefulness of considering anything that is not observable. Obviously, a great deal of actuality and reality is not observable and yet we must discover things about those unknowns if our knowledge is to advance. We do this by making refined assumptions—by formulating theory.

Skinner's work is enormously useful within a certain, limited applicability. It assumes, however, a mechanistic conception of the universe and humanity. It therefore denies such important human characteristics as sense of purpose, dignity, freedom, aspiration, hope, intuition, and idealism. It cannot account for the nine Beethoven symphonies, the great ballets, paintings, sculptures, and inventions of the world. In short, the theory is devoid of any capacity to explain creativity, and since creativity is the process of translating potentiality into actuality, the Skinnerian approach is inadequate as the foundation for an educational system. I take the pains to discuss Skinner because there are many people who see it as the solution to everything and there are those who deny its usefulness entirely. According to our own theoretical and philosophical perspectives, both positions are untenable. The behavioral modification approach to education can be understood within the framework of arranging environments and guiding the child's interaction with them. Because the approach is not developmentally based, its applicability has limits; but one would be foolish to deny its usefulness and therefore ignore it.

The truth is that we need more than description; we need explanation. If early childhood education is to serve children in better ways we must have an accumulative body of knowledge organized into a science so that we can know what works and why, and what doesn't work and why. It is extremely useful to know what doesn't work so that we can quit doing that and advise others to stop doing it as well. Einstein once told a colleague about his intensive labor over quite a long period of time on an idea which he hoped would lead to a unified field theory. However, the idea came to a dead end. Einstein then casually commented on the fact that he was about to publish all of this work. The colleague asked him why he would bother to publish it. Einstein said he was publishing it "to save some other fool from wasting six months of work on the same idea."

At this stage of our development, no one is very certain about what works, but we freely advise each other on things to do and we do not feel called upon to provide a theoretical justification or to give empirical evidence of its workability. (Skinner has done better than most on this score.) We need a science so that we can stop wasting time on things that don't work. We need reliable knowledge to reverse the trends in increasing pathologies of crime and mental illness and get on with the other pressing issues: disease, the population explosion, poverty, famine, racism, pollution, and war.

Areas for Further Investigation

The background I have just given you will help to place in context some highlights of the twenty years of research the Anisa Project staff now has before it. When we find answers to these questions we will have a body of knowledge about human growth and development far better organized than now. Education will have begun to emerge as a science. All of the questions or issues I will mention have been stimulated by the interplay between theory and practice.

Since the brain is the seat of consciousness and the place where most learning takes place, we are necessarily interested in every discovery about the human brain. Of particular interest is the issue of cerebral dominance. As you know, the cerebral cortex is divided into two distinct halves, and preliminary research indicates they may have slightly different functions. If the left hemisphere is dominant in a child, this may indicate one kind of learning style; if the right cerebral hemisphere is dominant, another learning style may be operating. More knowledge in this area would help us to individualize instruction more successfully to help children avoid failure.

We need a more comprehensive definition of intelligence which is as culture free as possible. Therefore, an area of research we have in mind concerns the use of computers in the analysis of the EEG patterns as one means of assessing intelligence. Too much of the present IQ score depends on the memory of given information. A child who hasn't been exposed to the information required, for whatever reason, will receive a lower score on the IQ test. Furthermore, standard IQ tests do not yield information on creativity, imagination, or intelligence in relating to other human beings. Much work remains to be done in this area.

Biofeedback studies have opened up an entirely new area of educational inquiry. That people can learn to control their brain wave frequencies, reduce blood pressure, decrease heart rate, and potentially control other internal functions leads to a number of very important researchable questions. For instance, could anxiety be made manageable through biofeedback? Could fear responses be reduced or eliminated through biofeedback? Could such things as stage fright, test anxiety, or other forms of intense discomfort be reduced through learning mediated by biofeedback?

A great deal is already known about the relationship between brain development and malnutrition, but we need more extensive studies on the relationships between nutrition, hormone production, and the development of the brain, particularly in the areas of myelination of neurons and the branching of dendrites and axons and their interconnections with other neurons as influenced by nutrition.

If we accept the basic proposition in the theory of development that interaction with the environment promotes learning, then we would expect different kinds of experiences to have particular effects on brain development. A certain number of animal studies in this regard have already been undertaken. We now need to explore a number of questions concerning the enrichment of the environment, experience, and brain development.

An increasing number of children seem to be suffering from hyperkinesis or minimal brain dysfunction, a general learning disability characterized by an inability to pay attention, excessive activity, unresponsiveness to punishment or affection, impulsive behavior, motor coordination difficulties, and problems with perception and reading. A growing body of evidence seems to indicate that for many children this syndrome is related to the ingestion of food additives: preservatives, artificial flavors and colors. It appears that some children have a genetically determined inability to metabolize certain of the complex compounds that are put into foods. If they are not metabolized, they accumulate, become toxic, and influence behavior. A new area of research, therefore, must be undertaken which relates genetics, pharmacology, nutrition, and toxicology to behavior problems and learning disabilities.

We need to know much more about the nature of attention and concentration and how children come to gain control over their attentional faculties. We do know that if a child is not paying attention, little or no learning takes place and very little is remembered. The nature of human memory has been the object of a good deal of study over the last twenty-five years. A more systematic inquiry into the function and nature of memory is needed, particularly as it pertains to the kinds of learning important to children in school. What causes forgetting? How is confusion related to forgetting? What kinds of teaching avoid confusion and aid memory?

The human capacity to symbolize makes us unique among all living creatures. The ability to create further potential lies largely in this capacity to symbolize. We, therefore, consider it a necessary object of extensive scientific inquiry. The study we propose includes language acquisition and the function of language and the arts, as symbol systems, in the actualization of human potential.

We have a need to become far more sophisticated in determining the effects of the environment on learning. One area of concern to us is developing instruments to measure the environment. Finding out the relationship between noise and fatigue and its effects on learning and sleep is of particular interest. Such instruments would be so helpful in making a scientific assessment of different approaches to education where particular arrangements of the environment are a prominent feature; assessing the comparative value of open education versus the self-contained classroom, for instance, will in part depend on developing more sophisticated instruments for measuring environments. Preliminary studies indicate that different kinds of lighting have different effects on the ability to pay attention and therefore the ability to learn. Certain fluorescent lights have a frequency that may be incompatible with brain wave frequencies and therefore cause some of the symptoms associated with minimal brain dysfunction. The same is also true for television. A great deal of research needs to be carried out to make a definite determination of harmful effects.

We need to know much more about the effects of mothering or the deprivation of mothering and the role of the father in building a foundation of trust in the baby's character. Trust, no doubt, arises out of a sense of security that comes from the quality of care given to the baby. The concomitant of trust is the capacity to take the risks necessary to explore the environment actively. There has already been established a positive relationship between the rate of learning and the willingness and ability to explore the environment.

Perhaps the most important area for further research concerns the development of scales for determining developmental levels pertaining to biological development and to the five categories of psychological potentiality specified by the Model. Once we can accurately determine a child's developmental level on all these dimensions, we can prescribe activities to carry development forward at an optimum rate. Such assessment tools lead to competent diagnosis and effective prescription. This is the basis for individualizing instruction, and therefore the means of equalizing educational opportunity. With such tools, we could make certain that every learning task a child undertakes is suitable and one in which success can be guaranteed. Use of such tools enables a school system to avoid setting up countless numbers of children for guaranteed failures, as we do now.

Julian Huxley wrote that humanity is the only repository of cosmic self-consciousness and that this has placed us in the position of being managing director of the "biggest business of all," namely evolution. The first concern in directing evolution is to find the way of guaranteeing our survival as a species and then improving the quality of life. The Anisa Model has a scientific approach to the education of humanity that functions as a responsible step in the direction of safeguarding human destiny. Its purpose is to further the actualization of human potentialities. That purpose functions as the primary principle which integrates all of the knowledge we have about human growth and development and translates it into terms that make it an effective guide to practice. Huxley has stated,

> The central overriding integrator, around which man's entire noetic system is organized, would be that of fulfillment-satisfaction through fuller realization of possibilities. (1960, p. 55)

By noetic system Huxley means "a complex of the sharable and transmissable activities and products of human minds, the patterns of thought and science, law and morality, art and ritual, which form the basis of human society" (1960, p. 47). In our view, nothing short of a comprehensive system of education that relates family and home to community and school in the context of humanity's cosmic destiny will be adequate to deal with the critical issues facing civilization. Such a system of education will surely have to have a scientific basis, but one that rests on a philosophy that views each human being as something much, much more than a material creature whose marvelous complexity is merely an accident of evolution.

References

Huxley, J. *Knowledge, Morality, and Destiny.* New York: Harper and Brothers, 1960.
Kahn, H., and Wiener, A.J. "The Next Thirty Years." *DAEDALUS* 96, no. 3 (Summer 1967).
Whitehead, A.N. *Process and Reality.* New York: Macmillan Co., 1960.

Early Childhood in Art

Bettye M. Caldwell, *Professor of Education and Director of the Center for Early Development and Education, University of Arkansas at Little Rock, Little Rock, Arkansas.*

The representation of early childhood that finds its way into our art communicates the artists' distillations of the science of child development. That is, the artist who creates an artistic production must, if it involves young children, incorporate his or her own unverbalized concepts of what children are like, and what their behavioral characteristics, interests, and abilities are. In short, the artist must communicate to us through the artistic production an idiosyncratic theory of child development.

A society's artists (painters, poets, musicians, etc.) will always mirror an age and, at the same time, anticipate the future and compress the past. We all recognize in the truly creative artist this ability to "see through" an experience and put into the artistic production things which we less creative people might not have been able to "see." In this presentation we shall take a brief tour through a few carefully selected works of art which have something to say about young children. As interpreter, I shall undoubtedly take liberties with the artists' goals in my attempts to deduce from the painting what the artist seemed to be communicating about child development.

One of the first things we become aware of when we look at early childhood in art is how incredibly beautiful the human

183

child is. Somewhat surprisingly, relatively few great artists have considered young children fit subjects for their talent. However, when they have, the results have often been overpowering.

Perhaps this neglect of the child as a subject tells us something about how children have been regarded over the ages and the position they have held in relation to other ages and stages of life. Claude Aries, in his book *Centuries of Childhood* (1962), reminded us that the concept of childhood is relatively new, having appeared within the past 200 years. Prior to that time many children did not live long enough for their parents to be able to expect to see them through the childhood period. Perhaps by "seeing them as adults," the parents fantasized that the children had already passed the crisis years. Because of this orientation, perhaps it is not too surprising that great artists of antiquity did not deal too much with the subject of early childhood. A clear exception to that would be found in the great reservoir of religious paintings. But reflect that in such paintings the holy child was endowed with eternal life, not the finite life of the earthly child of the era.

Early childhood as depicted by great artists recognizes the importance of the family, just as we do in theory and practice today. In fact, the family was considered so important that it was often depicted as a sacred and blessed group—the Holy Family.

As we moved along in time, however, formal arrangements of family groups were favorite subjects of great artists. Frequently all the people, including the children, were depicted as very austere and totally lacking in warmth and spontaneity. Many of us have perhaps seen family portraits on the living room walls of our grandparents that did not look too different. In this one (Fig. 1) I like the woman (an aunt, I surmise) who is laughing just a bit and bringing some warmth into an otherwise somber group.

In the more modern genre, families were often portrayed as very much a part of an industrial society, perhaps less formal yet still intimate and needing one another, and offering refuge and a sense of warmth and intimacy.

Other family scenes perhaps depicted the family of our fantasies—elegant housing, warmth of interaction between and among people, animals gamboling about the lawn, mainly positive interactions among the people who are actually engaged in interaction albeit with an occasional person pouting just a bit. Also implied in such family studies was the continuity of family life, with several generations engaged in the activities.

Characterizations of the family also had to deal with the reality of sibling relations—with the fact that children are quickly displaced,

Figure 1 Peale, C.W. *The Peale Family*

going from lap baby, to knee baby, to yard baby (to use the terms that various anthropologists have employed to describe these relationships), to no baby at all but rather to being a mother's helper with major responsibilities for the younger children.

Not totally lacking in the artistic representation of the family is the role of the father. Although generally in the background—if present at all—in the pictures of the holy family, the father frequently makes an appearance. In West European formal and American folk art, he was clearly the center of attention. Perhaps nowhere is there more impressive representation of the father than in this magnificent sculpture (Fig. 2) from the Vigeland Gardens in Oslo of a father vigorously bouncing his infants up in the air with all five persons greatly enjoying the event. An obelisk there portrays the family of man struggling to ascend and to evolve and to improve the quality of life in the struggle.

Regardless of the importance of the total family experience for the young child, within most cultures the mother-child component of the total family system occupies a very special position. To be certain, it has occupied this position in art as in life over the years. Throughout the ages artists have been fascinated with the mother-child relationship and have represented different aspects of it in their art.

Figure 2 Vigeland
Father and Children

In the first place, I think they have suggested that it is a holy relationship, one which is perhaps more special than any other of which humans are capable. Artists have often recognized that mothers are very young, scarcely more than little girls themselves. This beautiful little Madonna and Child (Fig. 3) by Leonardo da Vinci from the Hermitage in Leningrad depicts the Madonna as one who is barely beyond her own childhood, yet quite capable of engaging her infant in loving and developmentally appropriate play. We would have to assume that either the great Leonardo (who seemed to know so much) or the model who sat for him knew a great deal of child development. Both Gesell and Piaget should have approved of her behavior. She stimulates the baby's interest with a little flower that she is holding in her hand, possibly rotating it slowly, and she is holding it at what surely must be the optimal focal distance for the infant. At the same time, the baby has his interest completely focused on the object, and he reaches for it with a prehension pattern that is uncannily appropriate for his age. Furthermore, the mother is smiling, and when the infant grasps the flower in triumph, he will look up at her and smile in return.

But even some of the holy mothers occasionally looked sad, along with their infants, as though anticipating that not everything in the early childhood experience would be joyous and pleasurable.

Figure 3 deVinci, Leonardo *Madonna Benois*

Figure 4 David, G.
*Rest on the Flight
into Egypt* (detail)

Figure 5 La Tour, Georges *The New Born*

Some artists were quite careful to put into their paintings evidence that mothers understood something about the process of child development. In this scene (Fig. 4) we note that the Madonna holds a bunch of grapes in her hand to which the infant's attention gravitates and for which he reaches with his hands. Whatever the intended symbolism of the artist in relation to the grapes, the developmental theory is sound in terms of the child's early interest in objects and continuous rehearsal of skills of prehension.

But the subject of the mother and the child is so much a part of the human experience—and such a beautiful part—that artists were not content merely to paint a fictionalized holy madonna. They chose also from among more earthly subjects, as in this depiction (Fig. 5) of a newborn baby carefully wrapped in swaddling clothes—a custom followed centuries ago and recently "rediscovered" by more scientific research as having a soothing and quieting effect on babies.

The offering of nurture and nourishment has obviously been seen as a major task for the mother. This is true in paintings dealing with slightly older children as well as in mother-infant portraits. What is being expressed here (Fig. 6) by Picasso? That the child will not eat and therefore will not grow? Or that hunger stalks us all and that food may not be available for the next meal?

Figure 6 Picasso
Mother and Child

The artist has recognized that if children are to grow and develop they must be given food and they must eat, and that adults who care for them must play a major role in supplying that food and making the consumption process interesting.

Can this pensive child (Fig. 7) holding fruit be involved in a math

Figure 7 Goya
Portrait of a Child

lesson? "This is the big peach, and this is the little peach." Or can it be a social studies lesson, "I am going to share a peach with my friend." Or can it be what the Chinese would call a lesson in moral education—"I will take the small peach and give the big one to my friend." Whatever it is, the artist recognized one of the key principles of behavior modification—food is an important reinforcer for little children.

In mother-infant art dealing with feeding, it is gratifying to note how many artists recognized some of the valuable by-products of this remarkable experience—the eye to eye contact, the warmth associated with tactile contact of the two bodies, the kinesthetic stimulation, and the mutual and reciprocal pleasure in the experience.

We think of Harry Harlow as having discovered the need in primates for contact comfort, but when we witness the frequency with which artists have presented mothers and young children in actual body contact with one another, we wonder if he discovered it or merely labeled it. It appears as though artists recognized it many years ago (Fig. 8).

Sometimes artists depicted this mutual contact as having strong sensuous overtones. Anyone who works with young children will recognize their needs for frequent pats, hugs, holds-on-laps, strokes, and other types of warm touching and holding. Both children and artists appeared to have a good understanding of body language.

Occasionally the young child almost gets left out of mother-child portraits, reminding us perhaps that adults have their needs to be the center of attention occasionally, to wear and feel good in a new bonnet, to hold a spray of flowers sent by an admirer, to forget for a moment the extent to which we have passed our own youth. Even though the child, once born, is always there, adult needs occasionally request that the child take a side position, if not actually a back seat. This little boy (Fig. 9) was lucky he didn't get painted right out of the picture.

Also early childhood art reminds us of how much time is spent providing physical care for children (Fig. 10), keeping them clean, drying them off, and getting them warm after they have bathed, grooming them, and in general getting and keeping them "presentable"—again perhaps antedating Harlow by a number of years.

Not all artists have been interested in portraying the condition of poor families, or poor mothers. Daumier was one exception, and in this picture (Fig. 11) entitled "Third Class Carriage" he features a poor mother and her baby. From the physical accoutrements one can identify the social class, but not from the amount of affection shown the

Figure 8 Cassatt, Mary
Maternity

Figure 9 David, J.L.
*Mme. Seriziat and
child*

Figure 10 Cassatt, Mary
La Toilette

Figure 11 Daumier *Third Class Carriage*

baby. That is one characteristic that does not show a relationship with social class!

And Picasso, with his sharp and discerning eyes and mind, reminded us in many of his paintings that motherhood sometimes means fear (Fig. 12)—fear of the unknown, fear that resources might not always be available to care for the child, fear of evil spirits, fear of loss of self as the child develops. Likewise, we see in the eyes of the child early internalizations of those fears—a situation which we can see in the eyes of some children every day.

And is not the task of caring for the young child an exhausting one? Does not everyone who cares for a child occasionally want to sit down, hold the child in her arms and rest, maintaining body contact and support but nonetheless communicating, "I have my needs, and now I am tired; you must let me rest. I will protect you, but part of me I will withdraw unto myself. You must expect this of me from time to time."

Figure 12 Picasso *Maternity*

Not too many artists have recognized the beginnings of "herd" impulses that develop in both mothers and children during the early childhood years. The need to get together and talk to one another and share experiences, suggestions, ideas, coffee, complaints, and achievements becomes strong during this period.

Remember reading in child development textbooks about theories which described the child as a minature adult? Actually, a primitive concept of life in the uterus was that the conceptus was an homunculus—a completely formed miniature creature that simply grew until it was large enough to emerge, full panoplied as a small adult. Artists of earlier eras certainly expressed their implicit acceptance of that theory. The more "primitive" their approach to art, as was the case with American folk art of the seventeenth century, the more completely was this concept expressed—even to the point of not recognizing the developmental fact that the head of a child is proportionately much larger than the head of an adult. But the theory was also expressed in such manifestations as style of dress (like the adults), presumed stance, attention span, and the like. The theory of the child as a miniature adult was not valid, and art which reflected this orientation gradually disappeared.

Another important aspect of early childhood is the enjoyment of festivities. Children find great joy in such activities, and the realistic painters could not leave them out altogether. In art we find children doing such things as trying to learn to dance with the help of an adult who is able to withdraw herself enough from the activities to provide a little instruction; going along on a boating trip, looking happily at the man who provides the power, yet all the while enjoying the experience from the lap of a beloved adult; going on outings with the entire family to such places as the beach; getting to attend a wedding feast; snitching a pie as it gets carted by—or, if older, perhaps even getting a sip of wine. Such festivities, whether observed by families or by extended families of the children (as in schools and day care centers), provide assistance for the children in the all-important process of identification with adults which is such an important part of socialization.

Major artists have recognized that childhood is also a time of aloneness, of feeling occasionally that one is alone in the world, imprisoned by the realities of daily existence and abandoned by those who should love and support us, as suggested by this magnificent portrait by Andrew Wyeth (Fig. 13).

"Why have you gone off and left me?" "Why do I not have friends?" "Why can I not please you with what I do?"

Occasionally even the Christ child was painted alone, separated from the rest of the Holy Family, again perhaps expressing the inevita-

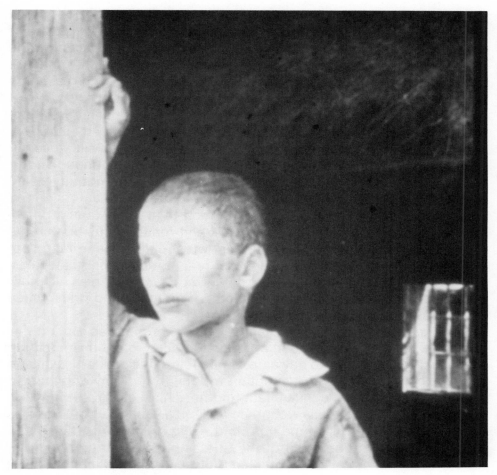

Figure 13 Wyeth, Andrew *Albert's Son*

ble breaking of the tie that must occur if development is to be complete, and that must begin in early childhood. Often the aloneness has a touch of sadness accompanying it, again expressing some of the occasional inevitable pain of the human condition.

Perhaps because many artists seemed to enjoy painting animals more than they enjoyed painting children (could they have seen them as more important?), we see much evidence in art of the enjoyment of animals which we find daily in children. Whether it is simply a child lovingly picking fleas off the family dog, or gently fondling a dove in preference to playing with the ball which lies nearby, these representations signify an interest of children which we recognize today and which we cannot afford to forget as we plan artistic daily programs.

Another aspect of the art of understanding childhood which artists have depicted for us is the importance of gradual exposure of children to and participation in the world of work—especially to the activities with which they can be expected to identify as they mature. In the art of the past we find a great deal of sex-typing with respect to work, a situation not likely to be corrected until today's artists begin to deal with this subject. Thus we see a little West European girl watching her mother sew or mend, a little Japanese girl from an earlier era watching the women of her village prepare newly woven silk, the children of circus performers begin to learn to juggle or get enough courage to climb the high wire, and an Egyptian boy of antiquity being taken along to learn how hunting and fishing are done.

More than any other early childhood theorists, Maria Montessori recognized the importance of work and reminded us that, in the planning of early childhood programs, we should provide many opportunities for the children to carry out real, not play, work activities. Sometimes they won't seem too happy about it, whereas at other times they might carry it out with a look of great joy and pride which says, "See, I can do it myself."

You might object to my next selections of pictures. But, in this chronicle of early childhood in art, I felt the need to get in something that specifically related to day care. Somehow, I decided, artists had to recognize the reality of this situation for children of any era. I would guess that some of our jubilant mother-child pictures depicting breast-feeding are actually wet nurse and child. But how could one be certain of that? Finally I found this picture (Fig. 14) by Paul Klee, which I included as much because of the title as because of its artistic or historic merits. It is called "Protected Children," and protection is part of what we must provide for our children in day care. I let my fancy run wild and decided to interpret Klee's picture as symbolizing the opportunity for day care to provide an *umbrella* which shelters and protects children. Note that one of the umbrellas is blowing away—a condition which appears entirely too real for children in America. Now they have good day care; now they do not. Of course, in all fairness to the artist, I think that I should comment that the children also appear to be protected by moral and spiritual forces—and definitely guarded by the ever-present adult, without whom no child is protected.

This (Fig. 15) is the picture that I thought you might object to. However, is not the legend of Romulus and Remus one of our first literary recognitions of the reality that many children need support and nurturance from outside the family circle, that occasionally parents cannot or do not provide everything their children need? This is substitute care of a sort that would definitely not qualify for aid under

Figure 14 Klee, Paul *Protected Children*

Figure 15 Roman She-Wolf (c. 500 B.C.)

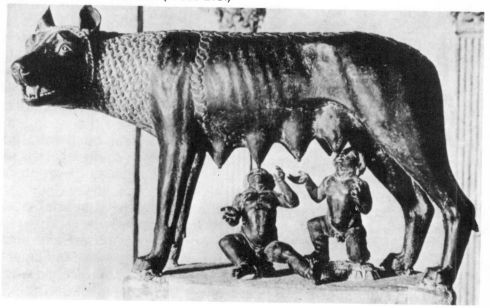

Figure 16 Vigeland
Motherhood

Title XX and that would not meet the Federal Interagency guidelines!
 Then, when I reflected on this beautiful statue (Fig. 16) from the Vigeland collection, I realized that mothers and teachers must sometimes feel the same way—as though there is not quite enough of them to go around to satisfy the voracity of young children for love and nurture. Perhaps it is rare for a mother to feel as overwhelmed as the woman in this statue, but I am certain that teachers often do.
 Artists and children certainly share one paramount trait in common—an active fantasy life. Many artists who have externalized their fantasies have put children in their paintings, as though offering the presence of the child in the painting as evidence that such fantasies are powerful and important parts of the human condition. *The Peaceable Kingdom* by Edward Hicks exemplifies this principle. It is as though the artist is suggesting that *if* the lion and the lamb ever do lie down together in peace, it will be at least in part because little children are there. Every creature, including the so-called wild beasts, must recognize the importance of children if life is to continue.
 Sometimes the fantasy aspect of art is not so extreme and merely depicts the child's fondness for carrying out wish-fulfillment and role transformation through fantasy. Lived there ever a child who, at some time, did not wish to be a clown? And Picasso's Pierrot (Fig.

Figure 17 Picasso
Classic
(Paulas Pierrot)

17), like real clowns, seems to realize that every Pagliacci sometimes has to struggle to hold back the tears.

The early childhood found in art also deals with such things as skill training. Here (Fig. 18) is a portrait of Picasso's son learning to draw. Note the toy dog sitting on the desk as the child works. Somehow we know that the dog is not to be touched until the work has been completed.

In the music lessons depicted by various artists, it seems as though the young child does not really want to participate.

All of these efforts of artists to tell us something about the early childhood experience would be hopelessly inaccurate if they did not tell us something about the mirth and joy which should be integral components of the legacy of childhood, such as being able to swing on a merry-go-round in the midst of rubble. Who but children can so magnificently rise above misfortune and disaster? And who but our artists can see consistently in our children the potential to do exactly this?

The great joy associated with one's favorite playthings cannot

Figure 18 Picasso
Picasso's Son Paul

Figure 19 Picasso *Claude and Paloma at Play*

be underestimated. In reflecting on this Picasso portrait (Fig. 19) of his children playing, I thought about how splendidly the artist has recognized the child's ability to convert a toy into a servant of fantasy and not be bound by the structural limitations of the object. Perhaps modern artists who paint what they see with the inward eye understand this process better than we as child development professionals sometimes do.

If I had to choose one work of art for this rapid course in art on early childhood—offered, I should add, by one who disclaims any expertise as an art historian—I should have chosen this magnificent production by Pieter Breughel called "Children's Games" (Fig. 20). (I bought my children this painting as a puzzle once, and we worked on it for months before we got all the games and all the children together.) Brian Sutton-Smith, who has done more than anyone else to call attention to the value of studying and understanding children's games, must surely have a field day with this painting, for the picture indeed offers a compressed course in child development.

Figure 20 Brueghel, Pieter *Children's Games*

Play is the true language of childhood. We observe children's play all the time, we participate in it if we are lucky, and occasionally we are able to give it some guidance and direction. We always stress that children need some kind of reinforcement for the things we want them to learn, and in this context we should never forget the automatic reinforcement associated with the joyful enactment of games.

But let's look closely at the painting, for in this we find compressed almost more than we want to know about children. We see their participation in group games, not unlike London Bridge; throwing or spinning a disc on a stick; doing a bit of role-playing, carrying around a bundle which is obviously intended to represent a doll.

We see group games representing a high activity level. Incidentally, this painting is from the historical period already referred to in which children were drawn as miniature adults and were dressed in the same type of clothing as that worn by the adults.

Brueghel understood that children love a great deal of rough and tumble play, often choosing games in which there is a great deal of body contact (Fig. 21). He also understood that when block structures are built or sand is available, arguments or fights might erupt. Likewise he realized that objects and equipment will be used creatively, not strictly as intended, as a barrel that can be a make-believe horse or ship.

He also clearly recognized the type of socialization opportunities inherent in children's play even when it was competitive—that is,

Figure 21 *Children's Games* (detail)

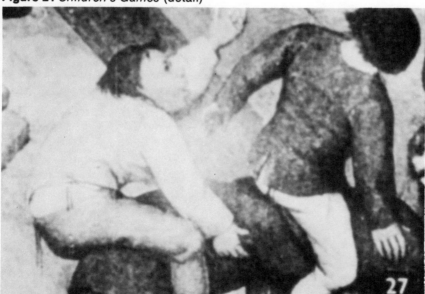

that children must sometimes cooperate with one another and become a "team" if they are to "win" a game. And look at the excitement associated with the joy of having your friends join in something you have begun, such as a simple follow-the-leader type of game.

Clearly he appreciated such things as parallel play—children doing things alongside of one another without actually doing them together—centuries before the term was introduced into our scientific literature.

Also he was aware of the delight with which children participate in large muscle activities—running, jumping, standing on their heads, on their hands and feet, rolling up into a ball, jumping and turning around a hitching post. The artist also recognized the natural diversity of activities that occur on a children's playground—though I doubt that any of us could cope with one quite as complex as this one. Some children in an area will be busily engaged in an activity, while other children nearby will be equally committed to a different activity, seemingly unperturbed by the neighboring events, although occasionally a child will suddenly take note of what is taking place "next door" thereupon losing interest in his own activity and redirecting his own efforts.

Sometimes being little is annoying, but sometimes it is a treat which means you can get carried around and babied by the other children. And I was very impressed by Brueghel's recognition that many, if not most, activities need a leader, someone to keep things going when interests lag and attentions wander.

Brueghel recognized children's enjoyment of small moving objects, like tops, and accepted the fact that such things are somehow more fun if other children are also playing with them.

Note the insight indicating that children will occasionally get into creative mischief—that is, remove the hoops of a barrel to use as play objects. Also he realized that a barrel is an excellent place behind which to hide for a game of hide and seek.

But I have saved for last my favorite details of this great course in early childhood education—the awareness shown by the artist of the importance of dramatic play (Fig. 22). What better setting for the enactment of dramatic play than a busy village square, where there are adults busily buying and selling their wares, providing ever-present models for the children. Here, we see the little children, make-believe shawls on their heads and a make-believe baby in the arms of one, moving over toward one of the older women who is selling something—obviously pretending that they are part of the enterprise. I can almost hear the giggles emanating from the canvas.

Then look at two little girls carrying out some make-believe

Figure 22 *Children's Games* (detail)

business transaction, exchanging imaginary money, and carrying out a scene that we witness daily in schools.

I always like to stress, as Sara Smilansky has so effectively done, that the dramatic play of children is greatly enriched by the participation of adults. On part of the playground a very elaborate drama is being enacted. I have adjudged it to be either a wedding or a coronation, judging from the crown on the head of one of the marchers. Two little children are carrying a basket of flowers which are being strewn in the path, while other sober-looking marchers adjust their posture to the importance of the occasion. But note that standing in the background, hovering over one of the children, is an adult, hands lovingly touching some of the children. In my mind she is occasionally interjecting a comment or question, such as, "Now what should we do after the herald declares the approach of the princess?" Or "Do you think we should be singing now?" Or in some other way working to stimulate a higher level of dramatization and a keener enjoyment of the play activity.

Conclusions

Thus ends this brief guided tour through a small part of the artistic side of early childhood education. But is not life always larger than art? Could we not draw examples from the realities in which we live of the same principles we deduce from great art? Such as:

... the beauty of little children;

... the importance of the family;

... the value for child development of a positive and reciprocally pleasurable adult-child relationship, and the necessity for awareness of the important components of this relationship in designing out-of-home programs for young children;

... the importance for children of fathering;

... the major role played in child development (even brain development) of nutrition;

... the importance of recognizing infancy and childhood as unique developmental periods with their own charactieristics, accepting children for what they are rather than expecting them to be miniature adults;

... the value of including children in the festivities which are meaningful to us—bringing adults back into the lives of children and children back into the lives of adults, as Urie Bronfenbrenner so eloquently puts it;

... the recognition that, in the deep center from which our concentric selves radiate, we are all alone and must face' our humanity and our human task in this condition;

... the value to society of encouraging expression of fantasy and the joy to be found in creative activities such as art and music and dancing;

... the importance of skill training;

... the need to orient children to the world of work to help prepare them for adult life;

... the need to provide care and protection for those who do not achieve this without our help;

... the mirth and joy and hope and optimism which characterize many of the activities of children;

... the deep involvement in play, through which skills are developed, with joy expressed through group games, competition, sharing, observing, manipulating objects, moving— always moving—and enacting miniature scenarios in life's important dramas.

Such activities present the élan, the zest, the excitement of life—the art of living, if you will, as well as the art of early childhood programs. There can be no "scientifically devised curriculum" which can eliminate any of these components which artists have intuited and which we, as program designers and operators, must somehow make possible for children. There is quite an art to doing it, but, if we manage, the result will be scientifically of great value to children, to adults, and to the total society.

Contributors to
Early Childhood Education
It's an Art? It's a Science?

Contributors to

Early Childhood Education

It's an Art? It's a Science?

Dr. E. James Anthony, Blanche F. Ittleson Professor of Child Psychiatry and Director, Eliot Division of Child Psychiatry, Washington University School of Medicine, St. Louis, Missouri.

Mrs. Barbara Bowman, Director, Erikson Institute for Early Education, Chicago, Illinois.

Dr. Bettye M. Caldwell, Professor of Education and Director of the Center for Early Development and Education, University of Arkansas at Little Rock, Little Rock, Arkansas.

Dr. William G. Demmert, Jr., Deputy Commissioner, Office of Indian Education, Department of Health, Education, and Welfare, Office of Education, Washington, D.C.

Dr. Stephanie Feeney, Assistant Professor of Education, Department of Curriculum and Instruction, University of Hawaii, Honolulu, Hawaii.

Dr. Elizabeth M. Fox, Psychologist, Child Development Unit, Children's Hospital Medical Center, Boston, Massachusetts.

Dr. George A. González, Director, Bilingual Bicultural Studies Program, Pan American University, Edinburg, Texas.

Ms. Polly Greenberg, Director, The Growth Program, Washington, D.C.

Dr. A. Eugene Howard, Professor, Early Childhood Education, Stephen F. Austin State University, Nacogdoches, Texas.

Dr. Daniel C. Jordan, Director, Center for the Study of Human Potential, School of Education, University of Massachusetts, Amherst, Massachusetts.

Ms. Eugenia Kemble, Staff Chairwoman, American Federation of Teachers (AFT) Task Force on Educational Issues, Washington, D.C.

Ms. Carol Phelps, Graduate Student, Department of Curriculum and Instruction, University of Hawaii, Honolulu, Hawaii.

Ms. Doris Stanfield, Coordinator, The Early School, Honolulu, Hawaii.

Dr. Donald T. Streets, Associate Director, Center for the Study of Human Potential, School of Education, University of Massachusetts, Amherst, Massachusetts.

Dr. Evangeline H. Ward, Executive Director, Child Development Associate Consortium, Washington, D.C.

Dr. Edward Zigler, Professor of Psychology; Head, Psychology Section, Child Study Center, Yale University, New Haven, Connecticut.

ONE CHILD INDIVISIBLE

Robert Carkhuff, James Comer, Jerome Kagan, Constance Kamii, John Meier, Patsy T. Mink, Brian Sutton-Smith and Burton White, as well as panels and other individuals are included in this volume. Topics include the involvement of men, minority concerns, children's feelings, cognitive tests and many other stimulating discussions affecting children's social, emotional, physical and intellectual growth and development.

1975. 283 pp. $5.25

Order from:

NAEYC
1834 Connecticut Ave., N.W.
Washington, DC 20009

Please add 10% postage and handling. Include name of book, name and address to whom publications should be sent. **Please enclose full payment for orders under $10.00.**

DATE DUE

OCT 9 1978			
FEB 1 7 1981			
GAYLORD			PRINTED IN U.S.A.